EMPATH AND PSYCHIC ABILITIES

Channel Your Inner Abilities and Unlock Your Hidden Potential. Discover the Secrets of Intuition, Meditation, Auras and Telepathy in a Journey Inside Yourself

Brenda Halliwell

© **Copyright 2022 by Brenda Halliwell - All rights reserved**.

This document is geared towards providing exact and reliable information regarding the topic and issue covered.

- From a Declaration of Principles which was accepted and approved equally by a Committee of the American Bar Association and a Committee of Publishers and Associations.

In no way is it legal to reproduce, duplicate, or transmit any part of this document in either electronic means or printed format. All rights reserved.

The information provided herein is stated to be truthful and consistent, in that any liability, in terms of inattention or otherwise, by any usage or abuse of any policies, processes, or directions contained within is the solitary and utter responsibility of the recipient reader. Under no circumstances will any legal responsibility or blame be held against the publisher for any reparation, damages, or monetary loss due to the information herein, either directly or indirectly.

Respective authors own all copyrights not held by the publisher.

The information herein is offered for informational purposes solely and is universal as so. The presentation of the information is without contract or any type of guarantee assurance.

The trademarks that are used are without any consent, and the publication of the trademark is without permission or backing by the trademark owner. All trademarks and brands within this book are for clarifying purposes only and are owned by the owners themselves, not affiliated with this document.

TABLE OF CONTENTS

INTRODUCTION 5

EMPATH 6

TYPES OF EMPATHS 8

    1. PHYSICAL EMPATH 8
    2. EMOTIONAL EMPATH 8
    3. INTUITIVE EMPATH 9
    4. DREAM EMPATH 9
    5. PLANT EMPATH 10
    6. EARTH EMPATH 10
    7. ANIMAL EMPATH 11

PSYCHIC 12

THE LINK OF PSYCHIC SKILLS WITH EMPATHY 14

CLAIR EMPATHY 17

THE FOUR "CLAIRS" 28

    CLAIRVOYANCE 31
    CLAIRSENTIENCE 33
    CLAIRAUDIENCE 36
    CLAIRCOGNIZANCE 38

HOW TO DEVELOP YOUR PSYCHIC ABILITIES 49

PSYCHIC PROTECTION 52

TELEPATHY 59

    HOW TO PRACTICE AND DEVELOP YOUR TELEPATHIC ABILITIES 60
    TELEPATHY ABILITIES IN ANIMALS 64

MENTAL TELEPATHY 67
TELEPATHY IN SPIRITS 72

GUIDED MEDITATION 80
MEDITATION PRACTICES 81
MINDFULNESS MEDITATION 86
TYPES OF MEDITATION 88

CONNECTING WITH SPIRIT GUIDE 90
WHAT IS A SPIRIT GUIDE? 90
HOW DO SPIRIT GUIDES INTERACT WITH US? 93
WHAT TO DO IF YOU FEEL CUT OFF FROM YOUR SPIRIT GUIDES. 101

AURAS AND AURA READING 102

INTUITION 108
IS IT POSSIBLE TO INCREASE MY INTUITION? 111
THE QUALITIES OF HIGHLY INTUITIVE PEOPLE 115

MEDIUMSHIP 120
HOW CAN YOU IMPROVE YOUR MEDIUMSHIP ABILITIES? 123

DREAM INTERPRETATION 125

DEVELOP YOUR EMPATHIC ABILITIES 134

PROTECT YOUR ENERGY 136

CONCLUSION 140

BIBLIOGRAPHY 141

INTRODUCTION

Do you wonder if you have done the right thing buying this book? I think that if you have felt the desire of going deeper on this path and discover more about empathy, psychic abilities and all this world, it means that probably you are a psychic empath and you just need to believe more in yourself and let your capacities bloom.

You are in the right place here, and I hope with this book, to answer at least some of your doubts and questions, giving you a little bit more of knowledge. Of course, there is so much to know and to say, and I already know I won't be exhaustive. You will have to constantly look further and search for new information, don't stop do be curious and to read more and more, trying to acquire as much knowledge as you can, to develop your gift and start to use it the better way.

EMPATH

An empath is a person extremely sensitive to the emotions and sentiments of others around them. Their capacity to identify what others are feeling goes beyond empathy, described as the ability to understand other's emotions, and become the power of taking those sentiments on, beginning to feel people's different personal experiences on a deeper emotional level. Science is split on whether real empaths - those who can deduce and take on the emotions of others around them - exist, even though many people claim to have such talents. We know that various researchers have identified "mirror neurons" in the brain, which may assist us in replicating the emotions of individuals with whom we interact. And it appears that some people have more synaptic connections than others, implying that empaths exist.

You are maybe asking yourself: how can I recognize if I'm an Empath or not?

First of all, an empath is an "Emotional Sponge": how much of other's stress or emotion you absorb? When you're with a friend who's sad about a breakup or very stressed for an exam, for example, does this stress or this sadness affect yourself too? Do you share the same feeling and change your mood?

Another peculiarity of empaths is that people come to seek for your advices or tell you their secrets, as they see in you an understanding and comprehensive figures, who won't judge, but will support and perfectly feel their emotions.

An empath is also a person easily overwhelmed: it can be a crowd, it can be a personal relationship, it can be something "new" happening, but you easily get anxious and scared for no particular reason in these situations.

Being an empath may often seem emotionally fatigued because empaths absorb everyone else's feelings - the good as well as the bad. But there are also good sides of being an empath, such as providing emotional support or help for others, and understanding better for yourself what is good or bad.

"Empaths are extremely sensitive, finely tuned tools when it comes to emotions" Psychiatrist Dr. Judith Orloff explains. "They feel it all, to sometimes an extreme, and are less likely to rationalize their emotions. Their intuition serves as a filter by which they perceive the world. Empaths are naturally generous, spiritually attuned, and excellent listeners. If you're looking for heart, empaths are the way to go. They're there for you through thick and thin, world-class nurturers."

TYPES OF EMPATHS

1. PHYSICAL EMPATH

Body Empathy is when you are sensitive to other people's physical symptoms and tend to integrate them into your own body. This extends beyond naturally contagious things such as laughing and yawning. Expect to feel strain in your temples if your companion suffers from an excruciatingly severe migraine. And if you're looking after your adolescent niece? You might get a fresh pimple!

2. EMOTIONAL EMPATH

An emotional empath is one who can sense other people's emotions. This may have a nice impact, such as when a buddy is promoted, and you can feel their joy.

But can also be tiring and complicated: friends that are persistent complainers, or narcissists who suck up the attention and never reciprocate can severely drain emotional empaths. As a result, emotional empaths are often the first to be exhausted by emotional vampires. Exercise self-care and learn to distinguish between other people's feelings and your own if you are one of them.

3. INTUITIVE EMPATH

Emotional empathy is frequently a component of being an intuitive empath, although it is not the distinguishing characteristic. According to Dr. Orloff, intuitive empaths can typically perceive the unsaid regarding what's going on, which can span a wide range of features.

Consider it to be a highly complete, almost holistic type of ability. "Intuitive empaths have amazing perceptions, such as heightened intuition, messages in trees, animal and plant communication, and the ability to pick up on other people's emotions" she explains.

4. DREAM EMPATH

Dream empaths might get intuitive knowledge from their dreams to assist them and others. This is because empaths are often excellent at vividly recalling dreams, allowing them to gain advice from a talking fox or a departed relative. A dream empath is also someone who can read between the lines an explicit message from their own and others' dreams.

5. PLANT EMPATH

A plant empath can properly "sense the demands of plants and link with their essence" according to Dr. Orloff.

A human who wilts with their blossoms and drinks with their houseplants isn't only the finest plant mom ever: he's also likely to be a terrific human friend. Offering affection to saplings can help you becoming more empathetic in other aspects of life, which is one of the advantages of being a plant-lover.

6. EARTH EMPATH

Earth empaths are similar to plant empaths as they both have their emotions tuned to the environment. While plant empath is more in harmony with indoor flora, earth empaths are more in accordance with what's going on in the universe.

"Earth empaths are responsive to fluctuations in our planet, solar system, and weather" explains Dr Orloff. "Assume there is an earthquake. They may sometimes sense it ahead of time. Or, if the Amazon jungle is being destroyed, it causes anguish in their bodies."

7. ANIMAL EMPATH

Animal empaths are the ones who are constantly at the party with the pet. They have a particular bond with animals since they can frequently sense their needs and communicate with them calmly. They can't accept animal cruelty and are most likely pinning vegan dishes on their Pinterest boards.

PSYCHIC

Psychic purport to use extrasensory perception (ESP) to identify hidden information throughout telepathy or clairvoyance, or performs acts that appear to be unexplained by natural laws, as psychokinesis for example. Although many people believe in psychic abilities, scientific consensus holds that there is no proof of their existence, and the practice is classified as pseudoscience.

Critics attribute psychic abilities to deception or intentional trickery. The National Academy of Sciences of the United States issued a report on the subject in 1988, concluding that there is "no scientific justification from research conducted over a period of 130 years for the existence of parapsychological phenomena."

But a psychic can be identified as a simple individual, who's able to see, hear, feel, sense, taste or have intuition beyond the edge of the physical, normal perception. Nothing mystic or paranormal, but more easily a person who has an awareness of the different sensory spectrum and perceptions, that goes above the normalized parameters. Psychic Abilities are the innate potential to process feelings and sensory stimuli on a deeper emotional, physical or spiritual level.

Most commonly, these skills are developed during childhood: we all know that children are more sensitive entities, with an innate instinct. But as we grow up, society tells us to stop being so sensitive, that ghosts are an invention, that pain is always belonging to something physical. We start to think and believe that this kind of behaviors and feelings are unnatural and not correct, not accepted by society, so we reject them. But actually, these skills and abilities are still inside us, hidden: it may require some exercise or tricks to get them out, but they are not lost. They are just there, ready to be released.

THE LINK OF PSYCHIC SKILLS WITH EMPATHY

While many people think that everyone possesses some level of psychic abilities, this talent can manifest itself in a variety of ways. For someone, psychic talent presents itself as the capacity to be an empath.

Psychic Empaths sense other people's feelings as though they've known them for years. They are acutely aware of others' wants and desires, and have the ability to hear, see, and feel them. An empathetic psychic has enhanced senses, emotional depth, and a strong intuition.

It is crucial to remember that only because you're emotionally sensitive, it doesn't mean you're an empath. Many people who are not empaths pick up on the emotions and moods of others simply because it is human nature.

The psychic version of empathy is not the same as the basic human feeling of empathy. Most people can empathize with others without necessarily becoming psychic empaths.

The primary distinction is that a psychic empath typically picks up on non-verbal, non-visual signs that another person is in agony, fear, or delight. Sometimes it is a question of detecting energy fields or auras; other times, it may just be a case of "knowing" that the individual is feeling a specific way despite the absence of evident clues.

Empaths have often trained themselves to sense minor changes in the energy vibrations of others. Most empaths are good listeners, and they tend to gravitate toward occupations where they can utilize this skill to help others, such as social work, counseling, and energy work like Reiki.

Empaths are generally very courteous and don't want to hurt anyone's emotions, so they'll often let others talk at them even if they'd rather be somewhere else.

Jondala is an empath who works as a nurse in a physical therapy rehabilitation clinic in Minnesota. She states:

"When I initially started out as a nurse, I worked in pediatric oncology. It was too much for me. I was so moved by the anguish and misery that I sobbed all the way home after every shift. I'm still dealing with folks who need my assistance, but I wasn't emotionally prepared to work in oncology because I was far too sensitive."

She adds that focusing on grounding, shielding, and centering has been quite beneficial to her.

According to Christel Broederlow, an empath and an author:

"While there is still much we don't know about how empathy works, we do have some data. Everything has an energy vibration or frequency, and an empath can sense these vibrations and discern even the most minute alterations that the naked eye or the five senses cannot perceive."

As empathy is the power to detect other people's sentiments and emotions without their verbally telling us what they are thinking and experiencing, a psychic empath frequently needs to learn simple shielding strategies. Otherwise, they may get drained and fatigued as a result of absorbing the energy of others.

If you feel you are an empath and are struggling to cope, try to allow yourself the luxury of some time alone. Many empaths are rather reclusive and being around others may be cognitively and emotionally complicated if you haven't shielded yourself adequately. If you're feeling depleted, spend some time alone to replenish your batteries. Allow yourself the option of reconnecting with nature in particular: you may realize that this is much more useful to you than simply being alone indoors.

Remember that being an empath is simply one of many different sorts of metaphysical skills.

CLAIR EMPATHY

Clair empathy's basic definition is "clear emotional sensation." It's a miraculous sense of emotional energy. Clair empaths are extraordinarily sensitive to the energy vibrations of people, places, animals, or things' emotions, attitudes, or physical problems. They may physically sense what other people are feeling and experience symptoms as if they were their own. It can also be like a transmission of energy between people, locations, or items. It's a type of extrasensory empathy.

Clair empathy is a mix of this empathetic talent and Clairsentience. The term 'sentience' refers to the awareness of a sense or feeling. It does not require rational thought, logic, deduction, or reason. It is, instead, a spontaneous energy perception. It might be felt as a tactile sensation, a body sensation, or an emotional feeling. Clair empaths see physical sensations as well as emotions in their minds.

Here some traits that can determinate if you're or not a Clair Empath:

1. You have an inclination to feel emotions or physical symptoms that are not yours.

Have you ever felt as if someone else's emotions have influenced you? Someone else's joy or displeasure might have a vibratory frantic energy that a Clair empath can feel deep. They may feel flooded by the enormous quantity of noise and opposing feelings in crowded situations. It can cause a sense of sensory overload inside them. Clair empaths are very sensitive to electromagnetic and subtle energy impulses. If this fits you, being labeled as excessively sensitive or melancholy may suddenly take on new significance for you.

When I was younger, I believed I was hypersensitive, but it was told me, in an discouraging way, that "I was just too sensitive or emotional." This, however, disempowered me and caused me to assume that I must be faulty in some manner. Clair empaths frequently feel and think they are the only ones in the world who are plagued with these feelings.

It's taken me a lifetime to discover my natural inborn Clair senses, and I now consider these unusual components of my personality as blessings. To protect myself from the kinesthetic overload that may occur while interacting with other people's emotional and physical energy, I trained myself on how to properly handle my ultra-sensitive side.

I now have a better understanding of the human energy systems and make it a point to set good energetic limits for myself. It took a lot of self-awareness growth and learning to continually check in with my inside and try to know what it feels like to be grounded or dispersed and overwhelmed. I've decided to eliminate discordant energies from my biofield and follow a daily energy practice that refreshes and restores my energy system to its full vitality.

2. It might be overwhelming to feel the bad emotions of others.

Inexperienced Clair empaths are also known to become introverts and solitary in order to avoid the confused and overpowering emotions of others. You become a natural protector, erecting emotional fortifications to defend yourself from the invading negative, aggressive, sick, and needy energy of others.

In stressful conditions, Clair empaths find it difficult and exhausting to be near people. You might get stressed and unable to manage the stream of incoming emotions from your surroundings if you are not proficient at regulating your hyper-sensory abilities. Having a discordant home life or work environment, watching unpleasant TV news or movies, dealing with angry drivers and road rage, or being in a huge gathering of too exuberant individuals are all settings that might overwhelm you.

I grew up in a household where heated tempers and bad emotional atmospheres were commonplace. It was tough for me to be around individuals who were furious, arguing or raising their voices. It literally made me nauseous and worried. I can sense the simmering tensions emanating from others, as if there was a dense prickly unpleasant sensation in the air. I experience heart palpitations in my chest, a tight, anxious butterfly sensation in my stomach, and throat tightness. I could get shoulder strain, an ache in my neck, or a caustic taste in my mouth. It has the potential to make my skin crawl at times.

I planned to be more of a people pleaser in most of my early life interactions, as many Clair empaths do, to avoid the disagreeable sensations I would experience when presented with conflict energies. I really like a quieter, more peaceful environment and was prepared to give up my own point of view in order to prevent any form of conflict.

Amateur Clair empaths are frequently targeted by emotionally insensitive narcissists, oppressors, and harassers. When I was in this circumstance, it looked like no matter what I did, it was a lose-lose situation for me. If I stood up for myself, I would be overwhelmed by the negative reactions these people would have, and if I gave in and did what they demanded of me, I would end up feeling bad about myself. This frequently left me feeling disrespected and wounded.

I discovered the hard way that setting boundaries may make people uncomfortable, but it is necessary for me to avoid feeling overwhelmed.

3. You are aware of the emotional and physical well-being of others around you.

Clair empaths are highly intuitive individuals who simply know things without knowing how they know them. They are able to detect whether someone around them has had a difficult past. They sense the energetic emotional stereotyped behavior that have been established inside that person's energy field. When you walk past someone or merely stare into their eyes, you may learn a lot about them. If someone is pleased or delighted about something, the Clair empath will sense their excitement and hope. When someone is in love, they will sense the intensity of their passion and affection. If it's something personal or humiliating, this might be unpleasant and unsettling.

Until you learn to regulate your natural propensity to be sensitive to other people's emotions, it can overpower yourself. I've sat in a funeral for someone I've never met and had my chest constrict, my throat tightens, struggling to keep back the tears welling up inside me because I was experiencing the emotions of the person tearing up while making a eulogy about their dearly departed.

4. You can interpret emotional energy from items that belong to someone, as well as from places that have an emotional history.

Clair empaths are more sensitive to energy residue left on an object or in a setting. Metal objects, such as jewelry, attract the emotional energy of their owners. Spaces where there have been celebrations or disasters, where strong emotions have been felt by others, will leave a distinct trace of energy that may be detected. When you enter inside an ancient church, you can feel reverence and respect.

As a result, the environment in which I reside is extremely essential to me. Having any form of bad energy in it does not work for me since I am compulsive about keeping my life organized. Messy environments "feel" energetically unclean to me and mess with my thoughts. I have enough experiences and emotions to get by without adding confusion to my mental clutter.

I've always liked to live in a less densely populated location since the chaos of city life is too hectic for me. Being outside and in nature feels wonderful and helps to cleanse my head. Plants, animals, flowers, trees, water, wind, the sun, and the moon all have a peaceful and joyful sensation.

5. You have the power to act as a human polygraph examiner.

Clair empaths frequently have heightened sensitivities to scents, sounds, touch, light and tastes. More significantly, you can detect how these things affect someone's emotions.

In my twenties, while training to be an interior designer, I unwittingly honed my Clair-pathic talents. I was trained to be aware of my environment and my client's interests so that I could design something that charm their tastes. Observing every element of a person, such as their smile, dress, perfume and hairstyle, is a skill that offers an amazing insight into who they are. I was taught to be a detective, as many Clair empaths are by nature. They notice and observe everything, even if they are unaware of it.

My spouse finds it annoying because I can generally tell when someone is lying. Knowing how to communicate and having a built-in radar system into how a person is feeling makes recognizing when they are lying quite clear to me. It's in my bones. Even well-intentioned white lies or omission lying will make me uneasy. No matter how hard someone tries to disguise their emotions, I notice something about them and immediately know something is wrong.

6. You can feel the psychological, physical, and other medical problems and symptoms of others.

"I know how you feel" have you ever heard someone say? If a Clair empath says anything like this to you, they truly mean it. You are normally far more sympathetic and empathetic than most others, especially if you are older, because you have most certainly experienced similar sentiments at some point in your life. You may also detect a person's true intention, making you more supportive and compassionate than others. When horrible things happen, having this sort of sensitivity might force you to take on the weight of the world. Untrained Clair empaths may experience sensory overload in doctor's offices and hospitals as they pick up on the worry and discomfort of those around them.

Mirror-touch synesthesia and pain synesthesia are examples of these phenomena, which cause the synesthete to have a comparable feeling to another person in the same place of their body. Scientific investigations have not only shown the presence of this sort of synesthesia, but have also demonstrated that it corresponds with exceptional or heightened empathetic capacity.

7. You are born with the potential to heal others.

Clair empaths tend to be natural healers, alternative medical practitioners, and emergency serve professionals such as ambulance drivers, first responders and firemen. In their areas of knowledge, they will act intuitively on what they know.

As a Clair empath you cognitively perceive the oncoming body feelings as an early warning signal and you are driven to do anything you can to help someone else.

People and animals naturally seek guidance, aid, or sympathy from Clair empaths because you are sympathetic and nonjudgmental. You appreciate an individual's expression of gratitude when they are assisted.

Being taught to properly control your own stress energy in a difficult circumstance would help to lessen the stress environment for everyone around you, both consciously and subconsciously. It's important to remember that we all, to some extent, react to the emotional states of others.

8. You have a strong sense of social obligation.

Clair empaths frequently have a strong desire to serve others, to alleviate humanity's suffering and to make the world a better place. Humanity's harshness or heartlessness frequently astounds you.

You are constantly looking for individuals in difficulty. You can't help but pay attention to folks who are in agony, experiencing emotional distress, or being harassed. This makes you feel in charge of the happiness of others and spur you to heal others or, at the very least, try to make their lives better.

By sensing the emotions of the group as a whole, you buckle down to ensure that everyone's emotional needs are respected. When you succeed at this, you become the person that the other members of the group want to emulate. As a result, you may be a natural leader.

On the other hand, you may be more prone to neglecting your own needs. You frequently say yes without considering yourself, putting the necessities of others first. Clair empaths who have received training understand the critical need of self-care.

"First, put on your own oxygen mask before helping others," is my new credo. Fill your cup first, then donate from the excess.

THE FOUR "CLAIRS"

There are in particular 4 "clairs" that Psychic can use to get information and understand situations and feelings: Clairvoyance, Clairsentience, Clairaudience and Claircognizance.

Clairvoyants "see" things, claircognizants "know," clairaudients "hear," and clairsentients "feel" things.

You can be naturally stronger in one of them, but everyone can also improve their Intuition and try new methods to develop the other ones.

Here an exercise that can support you to identify your actual skill level in the four "clairs". Don't take it as plain truth, but more as a tool to guide you and help you understand how you're interacting with this different psychic areas.

IN THE BEDROOM

For this practice try to use all aspects of your imagination, as far as you can. Make sure you are comfortable and undisturbed. Relax and enjoy.

You are now in a big, cozy bedroom, you feel completely at ease and well. There is a big glass door looking out over a lovely veranda and a forest. See the trees moving in the gentle wind, look at some little sparrows leaning on a branch and singing. You can feel the warmth of the sun on your face. Your attention goes back to the room, where you smell coffee and chocolate. You just see a nice breakfast board on a small table. You sit there and start to taste a nice slice of chocolate cake, the most perfect cake you have ever had, and drink your mug of hot black coffee. You feel the heat of the coffee in your mouth and the strong taste of chocolate together with his wonderful smell.

When you are ready, come back to the room, move your fingers and toes to bring your awareness completely back into your body.

Now answer the following questions:

- Did you see the bedroom, the forest, the sparrows?
- Did you hear the sparrows singing?
- Did you feel the warmth of the sun on your face?
- Did you perceive the heat, flavor and smell of the cake and the coffee?
- Was one of this feeling experienced more than the others?
- How easy was it for you to visualize the whole thing?
- Ho clearly did you see, hear, feel all the experience?
- Which one was the more simple, seeing, feeling or hearing?

- Which one was more complicated?

Answering these questions will help you understand which one of your gifts is more or less developed. The four "clairs" will be detailed in the chapters below.

CLAIRVOYANCE

Clairvoyance can be considered as the psychic seeing. It is the alleged ability to learn about an entity, individual, location, or tangible event through extrasensory perception. Anyone who claims to have such ability is referred to as a clairvoyant: "one who sees clearly".

Clairvoyants may see images of individuals, pictures, or symbols. These images can be something that has already happened, that it will happen or sometimes a metaphor of a particular situation.

Here two short exercises to support you in the development of your clairvoyance powers:

SEEING COLORS

This first exercise is simply about visualization, the first step for developing clairvoyance. Start with colors, imagine seeing the color turquoise, light blue, green, purple, pink and so on. If this seems complicated to you, you can buy some colored cardboard: choose one piece of cardboard, look at the color and then close your eyes. Imagine that color in the most vivid way you can. Try to become confident with this exercise of visualization, when you feel that you are mastering it, then move on to the next exercise.

SEEING AURAS

Start thinking of someone you know. Using your imagination, answer these questions:

If you were able to see that person's aura, fully colored, around their head, what color/s could it be? Then start to move around their body, and imagine which colors you would see there. You can do this exercise with people you know, as well with celebrities or politicians. Practice it as much as you can, with no kind of pressure: this exercise is purely for you and for your growth.

CLAIRSENTIENCE

The term "clairsentience" is derived from the late 17th-century French words Clair, which means "clear," and Sentience, which means "feeling." It's known as an intuitive gift or a "psychic center" in spiritual and metaphysical circles.

Clairsentience is the ability to feel the physical and emotional states of others in the past, present, or future without using the standard five senses of smell, vision, touch, hearing, and taste.

What are some of the "symptoms" of clairsentience?

You should consider author Glennon Doyle Melton's analogy of the canary in the coal mine when considering clairsentience. Coal miners started bringing canaries down to the mines as a preventive action in the early 1900s. Why? Canaries, as sentient beings, are more sensitive to toxins in their surroundings. Although the miners couldn't see, smell, or hear carbon monoxide increasing, they would be notified if the canaries stopped singing. This analogy is used by Melton to describe how empaths can sense and feel energies that most people cannot — and it works especially well for clairsentients.

Having said that, "symptoms" of clairsentience include (but are not limited to):

- Crowds make you feel overwhelmed.
- You frequently use phrases like "I feel" or "I sense..."
- You feel revitalized after spending time alone in nature.
- When you handle older items, you experience anxiety.
- Your instincts are your guide.
- You're an excellent listener, because you can deeply empathize with others.
- People may describe you as "overly sensitive" or "overly emotional."
- It is simple for you to read between the lines.
- When you are in the presence of dark energy, you may feel uneasy or even physically ill.

Is clairsentience a real thing?

It really depends on who you ask. Piers Howe, a vision scientist, proposed in a 2014 study that sixth senses like clairsentience aren't based on psychic abilities. "People can sense things they don't think they can see" he said. "However, this isn't a magical or sixth sense; it can be explained in terms of known visual processing." Finally, whether or not clairsentience is real is only relevant to whether or not it is real to you.

So, you've read everything up to this point and have a hidden impression you are clairsentient?

Start by listening to your inner voice. Developing your clairsentient abilities, according to astrologers and psychic mediums, is all about perfectly calibrate the connection with your intuition. You must be willing to "hear" what it has to say. Begin practicing this every day by listening to your gut when it tells you to do (or not do) something. Your intuitive communication abilities may develop into clairsentience over time.

CLAIRAUDIENCE

While in clairvoyance you see, in Clairaudience you hear. The thoughts or messages are in a prominent position for you and keep 'coming in' until something is done about them. Some people can actually hear these messages, as very short and straight forward. They sound like someone talking in their mind.

These sounds or speeches are normally not available in any commonly recognized perceptual range.

Clairaudience is defined as "the power of mentally experiencing noises beyond the range of hearing, believed to be created under certain mesmeric circumstances"

If you want to practice your Clairaudience, here an exercise you can try.

ARCHANGEL MICHAEL'S MESSAGES

Grab a pen and a piece of paper, get comfortable and make sure to be undisturbed.

Start by calling Archangel Michael and say: "What would you me to know right now?". Now, wait for ideas, feelings, everything that come up to your spirit. Write it down immediately, with no judgment. Then go back and look if there is something more. You can question Archangel Michael to clarify or expand the information you are getting. The only rule of this exercise is not to judge what you are writing. It's easy for people to think that they are inventing messages rather than receiving them. Keep practicing, and you will learn the difference.

CLAIRCOGNIZANCE

Claircognizance which means "clear knowledge," is one of the four primary psychic skills. It permits you to know something that is real or will be even if you don't have a rational explanation for it.

Claircognizants simply have an inner knowledge or gut feeling that they cannot reject no matter how hard they try. They just "know" particular things based on their own psychic sensations, which emerge as ideas.

6 INDICATIONS THAT YOU ARE CLAIRCOGNITIVE

Because there is a small line between having a thought and having a claircognizant experience, distinguishing between the two can be difficult.

Our minds have a habit of repeating themselves and are involved in keeping us protected and concealed. However, contrary to claircognizant messages, these ideas and instincts are not always correct.

People who have claircognizance may routinely know things without any evidence.

Do you want to know if you have this psychic ability?

The following are the six most prevalent claircognizant "symptoms".

1. YOUR GUT INSTINCTS ARE ALWAYS CORRECT.

We are all born with instincts. They are the result of prior experiences, heredit

y, and spiritual connections. However, unless you have claircognizance, your instincts are not always correct.

If you are claircognizant, you have the capacity to foresee events based on a gut sensation that has been regularly demonstrated to be correct.

Claircognizant people just know not to attend that party, accept that proposition, board that plane, or trust that very charming girl until they have a rational explanation for their feelings.

So, if you've recently known something that at the it reveals to be strangely correct, you are probably claircognizant!

2. YOU HAVE A RADAR FOR LIES

Do others consider you to be a human detector of lies? Can you often tell when someone is being dishonest, even while everyone else is duped?

These might be indications that you have claircognizant talents. People with claircognizance have a keen sense of insincerity and nearly nothing escapes their notice.

Even if someone is merely being fake with his or her feelings or emotional displays, someone with claircognizance may detect these insincerities.

This makes it simple for the people in your life to believe your recommendations or views about others.

3. YOU HAVE INDIVIDUAL IDEAS OR SOLUTIONS

Do you have unrelated thoughts or ideas that might end up saving you or a loved one from very significant consequences or repercussions? Then you may be endowed with the gift of claircognizance.

Claircognizant persons don't always know when their messages will arrive. You may be watching the latest Gray's Anatomy episode, driving your bike, or running at the park, when an idea or solution leaps into your thoughts.

Simply study them and attempt to figure out what your instinct is trying to tell you.

4. YOU INTERRUPT PEOPLE SPEAKING

Do you have a habit of interrupting others? Not because of discourtesy, but because you know what the other person is going to say? Claircognizant persons will occasionally answer before the other person has finished a whole statement, just because they anticipate what is about to happen.

5. YOU ARE CONSCIOUS OF THE OUTCOME OF A SITUATION

Have you ever been fully persuaded that something will happen but couldn't come up with a reasonable explanation? Did you previously know the conclusion of a particular circumstance, which proved to be highly accurate?

You cannot see the future with your five physical senses, but if you have psychic powers, you can. If you are claircognizant, your inner knowledge surpasses logic and reason, and you can predict specific events or results.

Those with this skill may form assumptions based on gut sensations and instincts that are often correct.

6. YOU ARRIVE IN THE MORNING WITH SOLUTIONS

Have you ever been jolted up from a deep sleep with a solution to a problem? This suggests that your intuition is functioning even when your brain is not.

It does not require proof to solve an issue and might just know the answer. This is a common characteristic of claircognizance.

This is due to the fact that your subconscious is in command while you are sleeping. If you are claircognizant, your powers are unrestricted while you sleep, emerging more frequently and so being accessible when you wake.

HOW CAN I IMPROVE MY CLAIRCOGNIZANCE?

Even if you don't exhibit all of the symptoms of claircognizance, you may possess psychic skills. Many persons who have psychic abilities must work on them in order to take advantage of them! It takes time to acquire and improve skills, but there are some relatively basic activities you can undertake to practice your claircognizance.

Here are three incredibly simple exercises you may do to extend your senses beyond regular awareness. From there, you'll begin to enhance your intuition and see and know things that others won't be able to notice.

1. SET THE INTENTION

Positive affirmations can help you develop psychic powers. So, if you want to increase your claircognizant talents, you must first make the desire to seek intuitive assistance.

Write down your objective and read it or say it out loud three times a day. Setting the intention and repeating it will bring you the things you've longed for, and you'll begin to enhance your skills.

2. AUTOMATIC WRITING

Automatic writing is another excellent approach to increase claircognizance. You will simply need a blank sheet of paper and a pen for this practice (or a computer).

Find a peaceful spot where you won't be bothered. Ask yourself a question and let your pen or keyboard begin writing or typing without conscious effort. It may appear stupid and phony at first, but have faith and let your thoughts roam.

Without producing or altering the words, simply observe them as they pass through your mind. Sometimes they won't make sense, but there will be answers that will definitely surprise you!

3. MEDITATION

Meditation is essential if you want to increase your claircognizance or any other psychic skill! It makes no difference whether you wish to increase your claircognizance, clairaudience, clairvoyance, or clairsentience: without meditation, your progress will be far slower.

You may improve your attention, reduce stress, and even become more connected to your inner self and to people around you if you meditate on a daily basis. With practice, you'll be able to create a state of calm and tranquility regardless of what's going on around you.

It helps you to feel calm while also raising your energy vibration. Spirit energy vibrates at a higher frequency, raising your vibration, and that's critical for increasing your psychic talents.

There are various techniques to meditate, so if one doesn't seem to work for you, consider trying a new style before giving up.

Are you a complete newcomer? You will find a special section in this book with more information and tips about guided meditation.

ARE YOU READY TO BELIEVE IN YOUR GUT FEELINGS?

Being claircognizant, like the other psychic skills, may be both frightening and beneficial, especially if you don't know how to interpret your feelings. It might be difficult to discern between regular thoughts and claircognizant messages.

Just keep in mind that the more you practice your claircognizant talents, the better you will get at discerning which ideas come from your psychic capabilities and how to apply them to make specific predictions. Just keep practicing, and one day you'll "just know" that you know without having to think about it.

For instance, if you have this psychic gift, you will quickly recognize when someone is dishonest or is not to be trusted, or you will just know that you must apply for that job. It is just understanding things without any solid support.

It might be irritating since others may not think you have this instinct! But you do, and it may be extremely beneficial, even lifesaving in some situations.

Claircognizant signals are frequently like a light bulb flashing instantly within your thoughts and then disappearing as quickly as they appeared. They arise at random and sometimes when you are working, watching TV, exercising, or doing anything absolutely unrelated to it.

Although claircognizant signals can be frustrating, especially when they warn you about individuals or encourage you to be cautious, they can present you with a wealth of knowledge and insights. They appear for a cause and might be quite beneficial to your life and its path.

HOW TO DEVELOP YOUR PSYCHIC ABILITIES

Here four steps that will help you to acquire or develop your psychic powers.

1. BE WILLING TO USE YOUR PSYCHIC ABILITIES

The first step in mastering this advice is just to be willing and receptive to tapping into your supernatural skills. You should express to the universe that you are prepared and open to exploring these abilities and that you will not allow fear to prevent you from doing so.

Fright is most relevant factor that stops a person from exploring psychic and intuitive abilities. People are afraid of their natural skills, but these things aren't frightening they're always there to support and lead us on our path and to serve as instruments to guide us in life.

2. LEARN TO READ PEOPLE'S ENERGY

Getting a terrible vibe from someone for no apparent reason is your psychic intuition at work, and reading a person's energy in this way is a skill you can hone. You should challenge yourself to interpret the energy of new people you meet by looking beyond their aspect or their voice, and concentrating on the energy they spread.

You may be wondering how. Simply being in their company allows you to comprehend your own views about how your feelings affect them. You may accomplish this before ever looking at or engaging with the individual. For example, if you're waiting in line at the post office, try tapping into the energy of the person in front of you and seeing what comes up. Then, strike up a discussion to find out which intuitive pieces of knowledge you picked up were right in the end.

3. PREDICT HOW LOCATIONS WILL APPEAR

The ability to feel and interpret energy isn't the only technique to employ a psychic sense. You can also practice psychic vision, known as clairvoyance. To do this you can try this remote-viewing exercise: the next time you're planning to visit a new area (say a new shop or a bar), close your eyes ahead of time and proclaim that you want to "see" this spot. Then, on a piece of paper, draw what you visualize. Later, compare your sketch to how the location appears when you arrive.

4. MAKE CONTACT WITH YOUR SPIRIT GUIDANCE

We all have spirit guides to whom we may turn for help. We're also connected to anybody we've lost who has gone over to the other side. Asking for a specific sign is one approach to connect with your spirit guides. For example, if you want proof that you're on the correct track, you can make a request to the cosmos, such as seeing a purple giraffe. It's better to be quite detailed in your request for a sign so that there's no doubt that it came from your guidance

PSYCHIC PROTECTION

Do you put your seatbelt on when you get on a plane?
Do you close your home door before going to sleep?
You do these things to protect yourself from outside events that you can't control.
So why shouldn't you do the same when it comes to spiritual work?

When you expose yourself to spiritual knowledge and psychic insights, you are opening yourself up to both positive and negative energies. It is very important to always protect yourself and your energy from all antagonist energies that can bring down your vibration and make you feel stressed or overwhelmed.

As we live in a big and expanding universe, when you reveal yourself to obtain deeper knowledge, there is always a possibility that you run into negative energies that you shouldn't absorb.

I am not writing this to scare you at all, but I just want to let you know the importance of protecting yourself energetically when you do this kind of work.

When you open up to spirits and access to different "worlds" you don't have to forget that, as we have good and bad energies here in our everyday world, so it happens in every other dimension.

Would you go for a walk alone in the middle of the night, in a dangerous district that you don't know? No! So why would you roam in different dimensions without any kind of protection?

Psychic protection is important when you do spiritual works as well as in your everyday life. We can meet narcissists or energetic vampires, overwhelming you with their feelings and negative emotions. As we are very sensitive souls, it is crucial for us to protect ourselves against this type of events.

Psychic protection can be of different types. It can involve shields or mirrors that deflect energy back to the offender. In other ways the protection is guaranteed using white lights or other color frequencies. Another way it's to look to guides or angels to intercede and shield us from mental harm.

Here two simple exercises you can use for your psychic protection:

THE MIRRORBALL

In this first exercise you have to use your visualization skills. You simply have to imagine and visualize an enormous, bubbling, rotating Mirrorball, that surround you. Any time a bad emotion or a negative feeling comes to you, the Mirrorball just reflect it and throw it far away.

ARCHANGEL MICHAEL

In this second exercise we involve Archangel Michael, an angel symbol of protection and defense. As this angel will always protect you and keep you safe, for this exercise you need to call him, out loud or in your mind, saying:

"Archangel Michael, please come to me now! Wrap your powerful wings of protection around me until I am completely shielded by you. Protect me from all negative or dangerous energy, Now!". Be clear and powerful, but never insolent or discourteous.

This are two of the most simple and basic examples of Psychic Protection. As long as you'll develop your potential, you will come across many other self-protection methods, that I encourage you to test and try.

Another obstacle for psychic empath persons is energetic vampires and narcissists. When dealing with this kind of people, or overwhelming people, you have to make sure of preserving your energies fully intact. Below some examples of how to react and interact in energetical difficult situations.

If you have to speak with someone you find overpowering, imagine he is separated from you by a sheet of plate glass. You can see and hear him, but his magnetic pull cannot be felt by you. Visualize this sheet of glass until it looks to be completely tangible to you.

If you have to interact with people who upset you but you don't need to speak with them, picture them separated from you by a brick wall and tell yourself, "You just aren't present. I can't see or hear you, and you don't even exist."

When interacting with someone who drains your energy, interlace your fingers and place your folded hands on your solar plexus, elbows squeezed against your sides. Keep your feet in contact with one another. You have therefore established touch with all of your own terminals and created a closed circuit with your body. While you keep this mentality, no magnetism will emanate from you. Your buddy will most likely complain about your lack of sympathy, no matter how well you talk.

If someone attempts to control you by staring attentively into your eyes, don't try to return the focus, since this will just lead to a tiring fight in which you may lose, but instead look firmly at the place just over the base of their nose, between the inner ends of their brows. If you're just dealing with a regular bully, you'll have the upper hand right away. If, on the other hand, your adversary is aware of mind-power, you may not be able to control him, but he will not be able to dominate you, and the outcome will be a stalemate. Do not try to control him; instead, maintain your gaze fixed on the location and wait for him to tire of his attempt to dominate you. You won't have to wait long.

Any person can stop an ordinary psychic attack; or, in the case of attacks of abnormal potency, can at least ensure himself time to hide and seek help by using the methods described in the preceding pages.

One last thing related to Psychic Protection it's Chakras.

Setting chakras correctly is part of energy containment. Your 2nd and 5th chakras are the primary chakras that allow autonomy and individuation.

The second chakra is the room of emotions and is placed two fingers below your navel.

The fifth chakra is positioned in the neck notch. It is the hub of great power and authority, as well as the seat of real self-expression. A sensation of powerlessness and weakness might result from being overly closed.

How do you activate a chakra?

Have you used a vegetable steamer before? If yes you've opened the steamer to cook your vegetables and closed it to store them.

That's a metaphor for altering the chakra settings. This is how it works:

Bring your consciousness to your second chakra and set the petals (the chakra openness) to 25% (you will be shutting the chakras' petals...attacks occur when the second chakra is overly open). Bring your focus to your 5th chakra and adjust the petals to 50 or even 60% (you'll be opening the chakra petals...attacks occur when the 5th chakra is too closed).

Let's talk about the aura now. The aura is a sphere of energy that surrounds your body. The aura powers your chakras, allowing you to live your life. Your aura is composed of seven separate levels that provide energy to each of the seven chakras. Each auric layer requires a border, such as fine net or filter cloth, to contain it and identify the energy as yours.

Your energy fuses with everyone with whom you engage, whether through psychic attack or casual dialogue, and with or without your knowledge.

Do you want to know where your aura begins and ends? Put one arm out in front of you and one behind you. Your aura ends where your fingertips finish. Extend your arms straight out from your sides, and your aura will cease at the tips of your fingers. Raise your arms straight over your head, and your aura will stretch to your fingers. Your aura reaches around two feet into the Earth as well.

Consider and welcome thin mesh or cheesecloth borders to encircle and enclose each of your 7 layers. Take a deep breath and pay attention to your energy containment.

Forget about psychic defense! Who needs an adversary? Set your chakras and auric borders to live in autonomy and individuated awareness by containing your energy.

TELEPATHY

Telepathy is the direct transference of thinking from one person (sender or agent) to another (receiver or percipient) without the use of traditional sensory routes of communication, and is considered a type of extrasensory perception (ESP). While the reality of telepathy has yet to be proven, several parapsychological research investigations utilizing techniques such as card guessing have generated positive findings. Using an unique deck of five sets of five cards the agent may simply consider a random order of the five card symbols, while the percipient attempts to recall the order on which the agent is focused. In a typical ESP test, the transmitter focuses on one card's face at a time while the receiver tries to recall the symbol. Of course, a screen or some other larger obstruction or distance separates the two persons. Significantly higher-than-expected scores are highly unusual, especially as testing procedures have gotten more stringent.

HOW TO PRACTICE AND DEVELOP YOUR TELEPATHIC ABILITIES

How can you "wake up" your telepathic abilities?

There is a simple method for developing the capacity to transmit and interpret thoughts.

You may do a simple exercise to determine how evolved your ability for telepathy is, so you can work on it later.

The approach outlined below will gradually strengthen your capacity to receive and transmit other people's ideas. Like a radio station, you will learn to broadcast and receive signals (thoughts and feelings) from another individual.

The possibilities that evolved telepathy opens up are just unfathomable and inspire the imagination!

Prerequisites for Practice

Two requirements must be satisfied for this procedure to take place:

- the presence of a partner (start with someone you trust, and later practice with persons of various sex, age, career, and religion)

- a peaceful location (where no one will distract, break concentration).

The outcomes of this exercise will persuade you that you indeed have telepathic abilities!

1. You must sit across from each other - the practitioner sits across from the partner.

2. Each person will require a piece of paper and a pen.

It is vital to assign roles: one will broadcast the signal, while the other will receive it.

3. You must relax, concentrate, and let go of all ideas.

This may be accomplished by just observing your breathing. You must concentrate on this procedure for a few minutes: take a deep breath and exhale. Soon, you'll be in a peaceful, almost meditative condition.

4. The practitioner initially gives the signal to his partner, drawing something on his paper.

What is shown on paper should not be seen by the partner!

5. The practitioner recalls the image and imagines it "rising" from the paper into the air.

6. You must focus completely on this image, seeing it floating in the air between the practitioner and the partner.

7. After that, you must give the image volume and color. It is sufficient to focus on it for approximately 30 seconds, making an imaginary figure three-dimensional, "drawing" the details, and filling it with colors, without losing sight of the overall picture.

8. You may now let go of a full-fledged figure: imagine that your partner saw her as well, and picture how the image enters his thoughts, into his brain.

9. Then, ask your companion to draw whatever comes to mind first (whatever it was). He has to draw that notion, that image in his thoughts that occurred at that very instant.

A partner can draw an aircraft instead of a bird, or a dandelion instead of a lush-crowned tree. However, the schematics will be identical: the same direction, same curves, dimensions, and details.

Ideally, the partner should be able to perceive the image in three dimensions and identify the colors.

Then, with the partner, exchange roles, acting as the one receiving the signal, and repeat the activity.

Important!

Don't anticipate immediate results! It's possible that it won't work the first time. The ability must be cultivated, which can only be accomplished via consistent practice.

The power to communicate mentally is inherent in all of us, since our childhood.

Training must be continued until a definite result is obtained, and then this talent have to be further developed.

As a consequence, you will be able to connect to people's broad mental backgrounds or the thoughts of a specific individual, as well as transmit your own ideas to others - telepathy will open up new doors and can drastically improve your life!

Methods have you perplexed? Are you unsure if you're on the correct track? Perhaps you were born with a proclivity towards other skills!

TELEPATHY ABILITIES IN ANIMALS

In animals, instinctive telepathy is easy to detect. The enigmatic migration patterns of birds, fish, insects, and other creatures are evidence of mass telepathy, the lowest type of innate telepathy. Rupert Sheldrake, a British biologist and author, reminds out that in the fall, the English swallow travels 6,000 kilometers to its winter-feeding areas in Africa. The grey whale travels 4,000 miles to the Bering Sea after spending the winter at its breeding grounds in Baja California, Mexico. Monarch butterflies, which are born near the Great Lakes, travel over 2,000 miles to the Mexican highlands to spend the winter. Scientists have suggestions but no definitive answers as to how animals manage to travel such long distances year after year.

There is also evidence of instinctive telepathy between animals and humans. This interaction, once again, is based on personal relationships. In his book "Dogs That Know When Their Owners Are Coming Home and Other Unexplained Powers of Animals", Rupert Sheldrake investigate this sort of telepathy. Sheldrake's study on the perceptiveness of dogs, cats, parrots, horses, and other animals is presented in this book. His study includes random surveys of over a thousand pet owners as well as interviews with hundreds of professionals who interact with animals, including dog handlers, doctors, kennel and stable owners, horse trainers and riders. He noticed that dogs and other animals frequently anticipate the coming of their owners, even when the owners return home at odd times or in strange cars.

Sheldrake conducted a lengthy recorded experiment with Jaytee, a mixed-breed terrier owned by his assistant, Pamela Smart. Pam frequently left Jaytee with her parents, who lived in the flat next door, while she went out. Pam and her parents began the experiment by maintaining a journal of her travels and Jaytee's reaction to her homecoming. Jaytee anticipated her return by waiting outside the window for 10 minutes or more on 85 of 100 occasions, according to Sheldrake, even when she returned at various times and by unconventional means - a bicycle, train, or taxi.

Sheldrake also documented more cases of human-to-animal telepathy, such as dogs that knew when their owners were planning a stroll and cats who knew when they were going to the vet. He also documented anecdotes about cats, dogs, and even horses who found their way home after being separated from their owners for an extended period of time.

A friend's story of a childhood pet, a Yorkshire terrier named Teddy, captivated me. Teddy spent his days basking in the sun on his grandparents' back porch in New Ulm, a little town in Minnesota. Teddy would scratch at the back door until grandma let him out at a specific time each weekday afternoon. He'd then trot through the streets until he got to my friend's primary school, which was a mile away. When my friend stepped out of school at 3:00 p.m., Teddy was usually there, wagging his tail in greeting. I was curious as to how he knew what time to leave. How did he find his way around?

Teddy, like Jaytee, may have been reacting to my father's anticipation of the last school bell. His ability to find his way to school each day might be attributed to the "morphic field" that connects people to their cherished dogs.

MENTAL TELEPATHY

Mental telepathy, also known as thought transference, is a type of mind-to-mind communication. The neck center and the lower layers of the mental plane are used in this sort of telepathy. Telepathic contact is established between two fully conscious, focused minds, as opposed to trance channeling, which is a sort of mediumship in which a disembodied spirit utilizes a channel's body to deliver a message.

Alice Bailey began working with Tibetan instructor Djwal Khul in 1919. When she was fifteen, she was surprised by a turbaned guy who informed her he would have job for her in the future. Twenty-four years later, as a mother of three, she heard a "voice" asking for her help in authoring a series of novels. She agreed with considerable difficulty. Bailey claims that at first, she merely listened and jotted down the words that were "dropped into my head, one by one." As their brains got more attuned, she was able to immediately record and write down the Tibetan master's thoughts and ideas. They published nineteen works on consciousness and evolution during a thirty-year span. Bailey was the person who popularized the term "new age."

The direct transmission performed by the Buddhist teacher Padmasambhava, who transmitted Buddhist traditions from India to Tibet in the seventh century, is another example of mind-to-mind telepathy. Padmasambhava was claimed to have hidden lessons, books, and holy items for future generations to unearth. The teachings, known as termas, or "spiritual riches" are mentally passed to masters, known as tertons, or "treasure finders," in two ways.

On yellow scrolls, earth termas are symbolic writings. These manuscripts are hidden in mountains, lakes, and temples. These symbols, if discovered, would rouse the terton's conscious mind to the guru's teachings. Mind termas are direct transfers of mind from guru to terton. These teachings are hidden within the terton's consciousness as letters or sounds. The terton becomes cognitively aware of the conveyed information at the proper time. These types of direct transmission have permitted the teachings to be passed down in an uninterrupted lineage from one generation to the next.

True mental telepathy is still uncommon. According to Bailey, in roughly 400 years, mind-to-mind telepathy will be the dominant means of communication. The first scientific investigations on this sort of mental telepathy were conducted in the 1880s. According to Dean Radin, the first research of mental telepathy was conducted in 1883 by Sir William Barrett, a British scientist. Radin traced the history of telepathic research in his first book, "The Conscious Universe", and described the most well-known experiments: Upton Sinclair's experiments with his wife, Mary

Craig Kimbrough; the experiment card tests conducted at Duke University; the dream telepathy experiments conducted at Maimonides Institute in Brooklyn, New York; and the ganzfeld telepathy experiments conducted in the mid-1970s.

I've given a synopsis of these tests below.

THE MENTAL RADIO

Upton Sinclair was most known for his novel "The Jungle", which revealed the filthy conditions in the meatpacking business and resulted in the passing of the Meat Inspection Act in 1906.

However, Sinclair undertook a series of 300 telepathy tests with his wife, Mary Craig Kimbrough, in the late 1920s.

Sinclair would make a picture and seal it in an envelope. Mary Craig would "tune in" to the image in another room and try to draw a duplicate replica. Sinclair reported these experiments in his book "Mental Radio", which was published in 1930. Mary Craig's accuracy rate drew the attention of numerous high-profile acquaintances. Albert Einstein was one such person, and he penned the prologue to the book, applauding Sinclair for his diligent reporting. The book also piqued the interest of William McDougall, a psychology professor at Oxford and Harvard who was regarded as the "dean of American psychology" at the time. McDougall was so taken with Mary Craig's skills that he established a parapsychology department at Duke University to investigate paranormal activities.

CARD TESTS FOR ESP

J. B. Rhine, McDougall's assistant and ultimately successor, developed telepathy tests with a sequence of cards while at Duke University. The cards, developed by Rhine's colleague Karl Zerner, were known as the Zerner ESP cards. The symbols on the cards were as follows: a circle, a cross, a square, a star, and an image made up of three wavy, vertical lines. Each symbol was represented by five cards in a deck. The sender would mix the cards in this experiment, and when each card was turned over, he or she would mentally convey the picture to the recipient in another room.

EXPERIMENTS IN DREAM TELEPATHY

G. B. Ermacora, an Italian researcher, conducted the first dream telepathy tests in the 1880s. A team of parapsychologists at the Maimonides Institute in Brooklyn, New York, conducted more controlled studies in the 1960s and early 1970s. A receiver and a transmitter were used in these tests. The recipient would spend the night in an electrically insulated, soundproof dream lab. Once the recipient had fallen asleep, she would be watched for fast eye movements, which indicate a dream state. The sender would next attempt to mentally transfer to the dreamer a randomly selected image. After then, the recipient was woken and asked to explain her dream. Throughout the night, this procedure would be repeated multiple times. The dreamer's information was captured, transcribed, and afterwards matched to the sender's image.

TELEPATHY EXPERIMENTS IN GANZFELD

Ganzfeld, which translates to "whole field," is a sort of experiment that seeks to replicate the state of profound meditation in which our physical senses become static and no longer carry information about the physical world to our brains. The receiver and sender are situated in separate, insulated cubicles in this experiment. The receiver's eyes are covered with Ping-Pong ball halves, while his ears are muffled with white noise headphones. The sender is sent still images or film snippets once the receiver has relaxed. The transmitter then tries to convey these pictures to the receiver telepathically. The impressions of the receiver are recorded and compared to the original picture.

The findings of each of the studies listed above - ESP, dream telepathy, and ganzfeld - were "statistically significant," according to Radin, and gave convincing scientific proof that this sort of mental telepathy exists

TELEPATHY IN SPIRITS

Spiritual telepathy, also known as soul-to-soul telepathy, is the ultimate kind of telepathy. The higher layers of the mental realm are used in this sort of telepathy. Only once we've established a connection between the brain, mind, and soul we can engage in spiritual telepathy.

We have the power to function as intermediates between the physical and spiritual world when we align the brain, mind, and soul. The Masters who control our planet's growth cannot have an immediate impact on life on Earth. Instead, they seek people who have a direct link between the soul and the brain. Information and concepts can then be "impressed" upon our brains via the soul. Once the knowledge has been anchored on Earth, it is distributed into thought currents that are registered by the general population. The deluge of intuition books in the 1990s, as well as the present interest in higher mental processes, are good instances of several minds recognizing the same impulse at the same time.

Ideas are sometimes delivered to certain people. Alice Bailey claims that ideas for a project or activity may be "thrown down into our brains." As an example, she cites the formation of the League of Nations, the ancestor of the United Nations. According to Bailey, the concept of an international organization dedicated to global peace was lowered from higher levels until it registered in the mind of Colonel Edward House, Woodrow Wilson's counsellor and confidant. Wilson and House were so close that Wilson reportedly said, "Mr. House is my second personality... His thoughts and mine are one." Wilson, who is sometimes wrongly attributed with the concept, requested House to prepare the League's constitution in 1918.

Another example of spiritual telepathy is Sim Simran's story, the publisher of 11:11 Magazine. Sim elaborated:

My life was collapsing and I was severely miserable in 2007. I was going through a terrible divorce and had recently completed a thirty-five year career in my family's business. I'd lost everything -my identity, my marriage, and my family's support. During this time, I began to see the numerals 11:11 everywhere - on clocks, car plates, and mailboxes - it happened so fre regularly quently that I began to believe I was going insane.

During the deepest stage of my melancholy, I awoke one night, glanced at the clock - which had miraculously just turned 11:11 - and immediately had a sequence of visions run through my head. The digits 11:11 appeared on a number of magazine covers, an online radio show banner, and a television logo. At that very time, I "heard" the words, "Do this immediately." You will heal, and others will as well."

I'd always heard that 11:11 was a "master number" related with the soul, and through more investigation, I learned more of its meaning. I took the advice I was given, and now "11:11: A Magazine Devoted to the Journey of the Soul" is distributed all over the world. 11:11 Talk Radio reaches almost 400,000 people each week, and my TV show will debut soon. My mission is to assist others in passing through their pain and discovering their soul's true meaning.

We become "God's arms and legs" as we learn to access greater levels of knowledge. We have the potential to bring heavenly thoughts and enlightened solutions to Earth in order to solve our time's most critical challenges. We may use the information we get to benefit mankind in a variety of ways, including as educators, humanitarians, healers, authors, artists, and business owners.

Our most prominent creative minds, known as geniuses or visionaries, have all had access to the delicate realm of the soul. The rewards of this experience may be found all around us, from the most exquisite works of art to scientific breakthroughs and technology that have altered our world. Many of our most famous artists, authors, scientists, and business leaders have documented their experiences.

Arthur Abell, an American violinist residing in Europe in the late 1800s, questioned Puccini, Brahms, Strauss, Wagner, and other well-known composers about the source of their creative brilliance. Their experiences are very consistent, as you'll see below. Each described the soul as a gateway to a universal source of inspiration. Ideas and pictures just streamed into their heads once they were linked to this source.

"The great secret of all creative geniuses is that they possess the capacity to appropriate the beauty, wealth, grandeur, and sublimity inside their own souls, which are a part of the Omnipotence, and to impart those treasures to others," Puccini stated to Abell. The supreme secret is the conscious, purposeful appropriation of one's own soul force." Inspiration, according to Puccini, is a divine force, a "vibration [that passes] from the soul-center into my consciousness, where the inspired ideas are born."

Richard Wagner, widely known for his Ring cycle of four operas, defined inspiration as the ability to become one with the "universal currents of Divine thinking [that] vibrate everywhere." "This global vibrating force ties the soul of man... to the Supreme Force of the cosmos, of which we are all a part," Wagner writes. Wagner explained his creative process to Abell, saying, "I see in my mind's eye distinct glimpses of the protagonists and heroines of my music plays." I get vivid mental images of them before they take shape in my scores, and while I am clinging to those mental images, the music... the entire melodic structure, appears to me."

"In my most inspired moods, I get definite compelling images, including a greater selfhood," Richard Strauss said. At such times, I feel as if I am tapping into an infinite and eternal source of energy from which you and I and all things flow." Strauss recalled a similar experience when writing one of his operas: "The ideas were streaming in upon me - the motives, themes, structure, melodies... in fact the complete musical measure by measure... I was absolutely conscious of being supported by a more than earthly power."

Johannes Brahms referred to his approach to music composition as "communicating with the infinite." Composing, according to Brahms, "cannot be performed by will power acting via the conscious intellect... It can only be completed by the soul-powers inside." He defined inspiration as "a circumstance in which the conscious mind is temporarily suspended and the superconscious mind is in command, since inspiration comes through the superconscious mind, which is part of Omnipotence."

Brahms adds: "I perceive clearly what is opaque in my everyday moods, and I feel capable of getting inspiration from above, like Beethoven did. Those vibrations take the shape of unique mental images... The ideas come to me straight from God, and not only do I see distinct themes in my mind's eye, but they are also clothed in the appropriate forms, harmonies, and orchestration. The full product is shown to me, measure by measure."

This has also been reported by writers and visual artists. "It is a secret which every intellectual man quickly learns, that beyond the energy of his possessed and conscious intellect, he is capable of a new energy... a great public power on which he can draw... by unlocking his human doors... he is caught up in the life of the Universe," Ralph Waldo Emerson wrote in his 1844 essay "The Poet".

While reading William Blake's mystical poetry, beat poet Allen Ginsberg had this experience. Ginsberg once told a biographer:

"I received the sensation that the entire cosmos... was filled with light, intellect, and communication... It's almost as if the top of my skull has fallen off, allowing the rest of the cosmos to enter my own mind... There was a sense of a fully conscious Eternal Father... in whom I had only recently awakened. I'd just awoken into his brain, or consciousness, a larger consciousness than my own... [It was] the consciousness of the entire universe."

Leonardo da Vinci and Michelangelo, two of our most famous painters, both spoke about their experiences. "The painter's mind is a copy of the Divine Mind," wrote Leonardo da Vinci, and "the painter has the Universe in his mind and hands... Where the spirit does not work with the hand, there is no art." Michelangelo, like many others, believed that his creative inspiration came from a higher source. "Every beauty seen here below... resembles more than anything else that divine source from whence we all emerge," he wrote. This message was said to be embedded in one of the panels he painted on the ceiling of the Sistine Chapel. God extends his hand to a reclining man in this artwork, subsequently labelled The Creation of Adam. The vehicle that transports God to Adam is an identical reproduction of the human brain, complete with spinal cord, brain stem, and pituitary gland - the brain being essential to our conscious experience of the subtle realms.

Akiane Kramarik is a contemporary example. Akiane was four years old when she surprised her mother by reporting a series of extraordinary spiritual experiences. She was raised in a non-religious home in the Midwest. God had revealed Akiane a vision of heaven, a realm of great beauty where flowers were the color and clarity of beautiful stones and plants could think, move, and sing.

She soon developed a strong desire to draw. She started with pencil seven at the age of three, progressed to pastels at the age of six, and shortly after began painting with oils. Her paintings, which currently vary in price from $50,000 to

$1,000,000, depict Jesus, angels, and other spiritual topics. Akiane goes out into nature to pray and ask for inspiration before beginning a new painting. Inside her head, the words and images appear. Akiane, who contributes a percentage of each sale to charity, thinks that God works through her while she paints. According to her, the objective of her work is to communicate spiritual messages to the world and to bring people closer to God.

I also discovered a corporate example of similar experience. Konosuke Matsushita, the founder of Matsushita, one of the world's biggest electronic industries, believed that his huge success was due to his ability to access *kongen*, a Japanese word that means "the root or origin of universal energy." Matsushita, whose firm brands include National and Panasonic, pushed his top executives to tap into the universal mind's knowledge by incorporating meditation into their everyday work routines.

GUIDED MEDITATION

Meditation is a simple technique that anybody can use to decrease stress, improve relaxation and clarity, and stimulate happiness. Learning to meditate is simple, and the benefits can be felt quickly. Here are some fundamental guidelines to help you get started on the path to greater tranquility, acceptance, and delight. Take a deep breath and prepare to unwind…

MEDITATION PRACTICES

Find a comfy location and prepare to relax.

Setting out time for formal meditation is a key step in developing a pattern and becoming acquainted with the practice. Even a few minutes each day can make a significant effect.

"Some folks grumble about taking time out of their day," said Atman Smith, a meditation instructor in Baltimore's regions. "However, practice is essential. It's a technique for bringing oneself back to the present moment in difficult situations."

However, when we stop meditating, we should not cease being aware. "The goal of mindfulness meditation is to become attentive in all aspects of our lives, so that we're alert, present, and openhearted in whatever we do," Tara Brach, a famous meditation instructor located near Washington, D.C., explained. "Not only while we're on the cushion."

Mindfulness meditation does not entail allowing your thoughts to wander. But it's also not about trying to clear your head. Instead, the practice is paying full attention to the current moment - particularly our own thoughts, feelings, and sensations - regardless of what is going on.

We've created guided meditations for a few popular activities, such as the body scan, walking meditation, and mindful dining, in addition to fundamental meditation instructions. "Each of the applied mindfulness techniques brings alive an experience that might otherwise be more automatic," Ms. Brach explained.

Even if meditating on your own is an important aspect of the practice, the steady instruction of an experienced instructor may be useful, especially when you're first starting out. Our thoughts wander so readily, and a teacher's straightforward directions can help us return to the present moment.

It's unavoidable: your mind will wander during meditation. You can detect new feelings in your body, things going on around you, or just being lost in contemplation, thinking about the past or present, maybe criticizing yourself or others.

There's nothing wrong with this; thinking is a normal process, just like breathing. "It's the mind's inherent training to wander," Ms. Brach explained.

When this happens, simply observe what you were thinking or what was distracting you, then halt for a second.

You don't have to return your focus to the breath straight away. Instead, let go of whatever was on your mind, reopen your focus, and slowly restore your consciousness to the breath, being present for each inhalation and expiration.

"Don't just draw the mind back to the breath," Ms. Brach said. "Instead, reopen the attention, then come and land softly again."

Inevitably, the mind would wander again after a few breaths. Don't be too hard on yourself. It's quite normal. What matters is how we react when something occurs. Simply notice whatever it was you were thinking about - without passing judgment on it or allowing it to sweep you away - and take a minute to return to the present and resume your meditation.

"The practice of coming back is where we acquire our expertise," Ms. Brach explained. "I'll be returning again and again." Notice it - think about it - and then pause, and then return to the present moment."

Here the steps for a simple and basic meditation:

1. Lie Down

You can sit down in the lotus position, as well as lie down on a carpet. The most important thing is that you find a quit place and make sure no one will disturb you.

2. Define a time limit

You can start with a short time, such as 5 or 10 minutes, and then add one minute a day when you start to feel comfortable.

3. Feel your body

Make sure you are in a stable and comfortable position that you can hold for a while. No matter if you are sitting or lying, the most important is that you feel your body at ease.

4. Notice your breath

Feel the air going in and out your lungs and nose. Concentrate on it, and if you need, at the beginning, mentally count the length of your breaths and make them become regular.

5. See when you "lose your mind"

Notice when your mind has wandered and leave the focus on your breath. This will inevitably happen. When you feel this loss of attention, just come back to your breath and concentrate on it.

6. Don't judge your wandering mind

Be kind with yourself. It's very complicate to maintain the focus and empty your mind. So when you lose the attention, just accept it, and try to come back.

7) Finish your practice gently

When you feel ready or your time has been reached, start to slowly move your extremity – feet and hands – start opening your eyes and take a moment to see how you feel. Notice the sounds around you, notice your Body and then your thoughts and emotions.

That's it! That's the practice. Don't worry if it may feel hard at the beginning: focusing our attention and let all other thoughts go, it's one of the most difficult things to do! Be kind with yourself and give you the time to train on this practice, as many time as you need.

MINDFULNESS MEDITATION

You may practice mindfulness meditation on your own at any time and from any location. Listening to simple guided meditations, on the other hand, can be beneficial, especially when first starting out. Instructions from an experienced teacher can help us remember to return to the present moment, let go of distracting ideas, and be gentler with ourselves.

Simply said, meditation is a method of mind training. Most of the time, our minds wander — we're worrying about the future, ruminating on the past, fantasizing, fretting or daydreaming. Meditation returns us to the present moment and provides us with the tools we need to be less stressed, calmer, and kinder to ourselves and others.

"Meditation is attention training," Ms. Brach explained. "It helps us arrive in the present moment in a balanced and clear manner by allowing us to move out of distracting thought."

There are several styles of meditation. Most faiths have contemplative traditions, and there are several secular methods of meditation as well. However, mindfulness meditation has grown in popularity in recent years.

The practice of paying attention to the present moment with an accepting, non-judgmental attitude is the foundation of basic mindfulness meditation. The objective is not to cease thinking or to clear one's thoughts. The aim is to pay attention to your physical sensations, thoughts, and feelings so that you can distinguish them more clearly, without making so many suppositions or making up tales.

It's a deceptively easy exercise: just be present in the moment, without fantasizing. However, with practice, it may produce substantial consequences, giving us better control over our behaviors and allowing us to be more compassionate and equanimous even in stressful situations. With practice, mindfulness meditation can even help us better understand what causes stress and what we can do to alleviate it.

Mindfulness meditation originates from Buddhist tradition Today it's considered as a secular practice that help stress reduction, cultivation of attention and creation of tranquility.

"There's a common misperception that mindfulness is religious" Mr. Smith says. "What we need to clarify is that it's a stress-reduction strategy and a means to psychologically strengthen oneself. It's a form of self-care."

There is a growing corpus of research identifying the measurable impacts of mindfulness on the body and brain, and it is gaining popularity in professional contexts such as education, sports, business, and even the military.

TYPES OF MEDITATION

Though the terms are commonly used interchangeably, there is a distinction to be made between mindfulness and meditation.

Mindfulness is a state of being characterized by the sensation of being awake and aware in the present moment, free of reflexive judgment, instinctive criticism, or mind wandering.

Mindfulness Meditation is the discipline of being fully present in the moment, which educates us to be more aware throughout the day, especially in stressful times.

"Mindfulness is your awareness of what's going on in the current moment without any judgement," Ms. Brach says "Meditation is the practice of training one's attention in order to achieve awareness."

Mindfulness meditation is not the only method of meditation.

Transcendental Meditation, tries to generate a state of calm and awareness via the recitation of a mantra, is also becoming increasingly popular.

Focused Meditation, is a way of focusing your attention on an object, a sound or an image, instead of clearing your mind with no focal point. You can for example focus your attention on the flame of a candle, or on the rhythm of a metronome: this will keep you in the present moment, allowing you to take a distance from your inner dialogue.

Movement Meditation, like tai chi or yoga practice, is an active way of meditating, in which you can create a deeper connection between your body and the present moment.

Visualization Meditation is the practice of finding relax and calm by visualizing positive images or situation.

CONNECTING WITH SPIRIT GUIDE

WHAT IS A SPIRIT GUIDE?

A Spirit Guide is a nonphysical being assigned to guide us to reach our best potential on Earth

Some spirit guides have been with you from the beginning of time, even before you were born. Others arrive when you need them at various points in your life.

Your spiritual guidance team, or the group of spirit guides given to you, may contain any or all of the following:

ARCHANGELS

Archangels are angelic leaders with a tremendous, massive energy signature. If you're an empath or sensitive to energy, you could notice an energy shift in the room when you summon an archangel. Each archangel has a specialization, like as healing or protection, and may work with a large number of humans at the same time.

GUARDIAN ANGELS

Guardian angels are only yours, and every one of us has more than one. Guardian angels have dedicated their life to assisting you alone. You can contact them at any moment for instant assistance. They will always adore you unconditionally. Angels are non-denominational and work with individuals of all faiths and spiritual beliefs.

SPIRIT ANIMALS

Spirit animals might be a pet who died and is now a member of your spiritual guiding team. Spirit animals may also be any animal that has something to teach you, such as a peacock teaching you the value of beauty or proudly claiming your abilities, or a wolf teaching you the value of having your survival.

Spirit animals may first appear in a dream, in your backyard, or on a coworker's coffee mug.

ASCENDED MASTERS

Ascended masters such as Buddha and Mother Mary were once human beings on journeys of profound spiritual growth and impact. They now hold a particular place in the spirit world as leaders and guides or tutors to humans like you.

All ascended masters are partners who work in peace, regardless of what society or religion they were a part of while living.

LOVED ONES WHO HAVE DIED

Loved ones or family members who have passed away may decide to be one of your spirit guides and proactively assist you from Heaven by sending job chances or taking care of your relationships.

Whether you knew her well or not, one of your grandmothers might be a significant spirit guide for you.

In fact, any human who has died might serve as a spirit guide for you. If you're a musician, you could have a spirit guide on your team who used to be a musician and performer himself and now wants to assist lead and inspire you as an artist.

HOW DO SPIRIT GUIDES INTERACT WITH US?

Spirit guides will frequently enter your life by providing you with signs, which are also known as synchronicities. "A significant coincidence," according to Carl Jung, is what synchronicity is.

For example, suppose you realize you need to strengthen your love relationship after a disagreement with your spouse before sleep, and the next day you spot a book about communication in romantic relationships resting on a coworker's desk.

Spirit guides may also communicate with you by numbers or number sequences such as 11.11, or you may have a lucky number, and when you go for an important audition, your lucky number is in the address.

Spirit guides may communicate with you through musical messages, such as a song that always motivate you playing on the radio as you get in the car after a long day.

Spirit guides may send you a dream with advice on how to handle a problem, or a guide may come to you in a dream.

Spirit guides may also send you helpful people and opportunities, which is another form of communication that often requires you to take actions (asking an interesting new person in your life out to lunch, purchasing a ticket to a motivational workshop) in relation to the person or opportunity your guide has sent or put on your radar.

Here are some techniques to begin connecting with your spirit guides and identify their indicators and synchronicities.

1. MAKE AN EFFORT TO BE MORE PRESENT IN YOUR DAILY LIFE.

Recognizing the messages your spirit guides are already sending is part of receiving greater advice from them. Many times, the signals our guides tell us go unnoticed because our lives or brains are too busy.

Action step: If possible, try to free up some time in your agenda or delegate certain tasks. You'll hear more messages from your guides when you're not racing. Try a meditation practice that works for you to help you calm your mind and upgrade your capacity to create more space between your ideas.

2. BE ON THE ALERT FOR INDICATIONS FROM YOUR GUIDES EVERY DAY.

The more you look for indications from your guidance, the more you'll identify them. But something else remarkable happens as well: when your guides perceive that you are becoming more conscious of them and their beneficial messages, they will send you more.

Action step: Remind yourself on your way to work, on the car or while taking a bath, that your guides are giving you signs every day. If you're attempting to make a huge choice, or if you're going through a lot of changes or obstacles, pay attention and you will notice that your spirit guide will come with more assistance to help you through the issue.

3. CREATE A NOTEBOOK FOR YOUR SPIRIT GUIDE.

Make a dedicated notebook just for boosting communication between you and your guidance. This is a holy space where you may compose a message to your guides and ask for special assistance.

While your guides are very close to you and your life, it may be quite effective to exercise your free will to ask for aid and direction. You may also use this notebook to keep track of any significant hint they deliver.

Action step: At the start of the week, write a letter to your guides in which you express thanks for something in your life that you believe they have lately assisted you with.

Then, with some words, ask for their support or guidance on a specific subject.. Keep an eye out for synchronicities from your guides, addressing this subject for the remainder of the week.

4. GET TO KNOW YOUR GUIDES AND NAME THEM.

You may give one of your guardian angels a name you've always wished for, such as Amy. Or you may be thinking of your guardian angel while reading a name in a book, such as Tony or Anastasia, and that name becomes their name.

Giving a guide a name makes them feel more genuine, which may motivate you to communicate with them more frequently. You may also get to know the personality of one of your guides after working with them for a while.

Action step: See whether a name for one of your guides comes to you through intuition or synchronicity, or go creative and give them a name.

If a guide is always giving you assistance in bringing your job to the next level, they may be sincere and driven. Another guide may be more fun and always provide you with hilarious advice, pushing you to loosen up and enjoy.

5. GIVE SOMETHING TO YOUR GUIDES.

When you're unhappy with a situation, unsure of next step, or feel like you are not controlling a circumstance , turn it over to your guides. Even if it's only to give yourself a break. This can allow new ideas to come to you as well as provide your guides greater freedom to conduct their work and assist you.

Action step: Experiment with energetically relinquishing an issue to your guides, even if just briefly. Instead of scheming and fretting, try to relax your thoughts. Use a mantra such, "I'm handing over this problem to my guides to see what they can accomplish."

6. FIND OUT MORE ABOUT SPIRIT GUIDES.

Simple researches about spirit guides will help you communicate with them more successfully. Look for expertise and knowledge that is good, powerful, and therapeutic to you.

Action step: Take part a course, attend an online class, or read a book about spirit guides. Consider that only learning more about them opens the door to a greater dialogue. Your advisors will be overjoyed that you are paying attention to them!

7. DEVELOP YOUR INSTINCTS.

Everyone possesses intuition, and with study and effort, everyone can grow their intuition. There are four basic intuitive paths that you may experiment with and develop.

Guidance can be heard as soothing voices in your mind (clairaudience), seen as images in your mind (clairvoyance), known as breakthrough ideas or mental downloads (clair cognizance), or felt as energy, emotions, or bodily sensations (clairsentience).

Action step: Practice utilizing your intuition to make little decisions that don't have a large impact, such as where to go for lunch with a coworker. You may also play a game with your intuition straight away by asking it which approach here you should highlight in order to interact with your spirit guides more effectively. Request a number between 1 and 10. Did you hear a number, visualize a number, have a strong consciousness about a number as a thought, or feel inclined to a certain number as you read through this list?

8. ESTABLISH SPIRITUAL PRACTICES ON A DAILY, WEEKLY, OR MONTHLY BASIS.

Spirit guides are from the spirit realm and have the great capacity to anchor you in your spirituality or assist you in discovering it.

Regular spiritual activities, such as creating a meditation table, participating to a yoga class twice a week, or take part in a spiritual meeting with other people, will foster greater closeness with your spirit guides.

Action step: Do something in the coming weeks, lighting candles or burning sage, to establish more regular spiritual practices in your daily life.

Try also to make a list of some of your most crucial spiritual credence. For example, you may believe that the soul lingers on after the body dies, or you may feel more connected to Spirit when you spend time in nature.

9. SIMPLY SEND A THOUGHT MESSAGE TO YOUR GUIDES.

This may appear to be the fastest and easiest way to communicate with your spirit guides, but it actually works. You can offer a real prayer or blessing, or simply tell them what you really need through your thoughts.

Action Step: As soon as you finish reading this chapter, ask your spirit guides for assistance in your thoughts about something you've been concerned about. Then, enlist the assistance of a loved one, coworker, expert, or health care professional. You are deserving of all the assistance you require!

10. MAKE SURE YOU USE A DIVINATION INSTRUMENT.

Since humans have existed, they have used divination tools to find a connect with Spirits. There are several divination instruments, such as oracle cards, tarot cards, and runes. Experiment with several ways to find which ones work best for you.

Action Step: To focus yourself before working with your divination equipment, take your tarots or any other tool in your hands and hold them for a couple of minutes, closing your eyes and taking a deep breath. Then, quietly request that your spirit guides offer you a beneficial, healing message using this instrument.

WHAT TO DO IF YOU FEEL CUT OFF FROM YOUR SPIRIT GUIDES.

Don't be concerned if you're feeling detached from Spirit Guides. You have and will always have a connection with them. Either if you notice them or not, your Spirit Guides are there and helping and supporting you. Sometimes we feel separated from them during the most difficult periods in our lives, but this is when Spirit Guides can and wants to aid us more than ever.

It might assist to keep you well-grounded while you're going through huge changes to feel connected to your spirituality and your Spirit Guides. Every night before going to bed, spend 30 minutes reading an inspirational book about spirituality, or watching a documentary or a movie on this theme.

Your Spirit Guides deeply desire a closer relationship with you. You may be agreeably amaze by how many messages you detect when you open up to them and try to communicate with them more. Your Spirit Guides have already sent you several messages, open your eyes and your mind and don't be afraid of listening and be supported.

AURAS AND AURA READING

Auras are defined as the invisible sphere of energy that surrounds a person's physical body. They are influenced by our mood and mental state (as well as the states of others), and various colors are connected with various traits and emotions. A person's aura is generally a rainbow of hues, with one color dominating over the others.

You may have your aura photographed during an aura reading, take a fast aura quiz, or try to identify it yourself by staring gently at anywhere on your body or massage your hands together, gradually separate them, and looking for colors.

Each of the seven chakras are also connected with a color, therefore knowing the chakra colors might help you read auras.

The following are ten aura hues and their meanings:

RED

If you have red in your aura, you are most likely an enthusiastic and hot-blooded person. A person with a red aura is "rapid at putting thoughts into acts" and "doesn't read instruction manuals."

Red is associated with the root chakra, and if you see a lot of it, it signifies you are well anchored. This chakra is about security and power base.

ORANGE

The sacral chakra, which governs imagination and sexual power, is associated with an orange glow. The appearance of orange in the aura may represent the flow of creative energy.

Furthermore, if orange appears in your aura, it may indicate that you "tend to acquire lessons through experience rather than theory" and "frequently have to learn things the hard way."

The orange chakra is located just below the navel, at the center of the lower belly, or if you turn back, in the lumbar vertebrae. This chakra deals with genitals, lymphatic and circulatory system, kidney, large intestines, lower back and abdominal region.

YELLOW

Yellow auras, as you might expect from such a joyful color, represent someone who is bright and engaging. They may also have a captivating personality that pull out other people from their individual paths.

Yellow in your aura indicates that you're feeling optimistic and strengthful.

Yellow is the hue of the solar plexus chakra, which governs your identity and self-esteem. When it is well balanced, you are motivated, purposefulness and full of energy; on the other way when this chakra is unbalanced you will become more aggressive and your self-esteem may be low.

GREEN

Green is one of the colors connected with the heart chakra, hence it is related with things of the heart, such as love for oneself and others, compassion, and forgiveness.

This is the chakra of empathy, unconditional love, forgiveness, compassion, acceptance and truth.

If you have green in your aura, you probably enjoy "music, nature, and not being tied down." Because a green aura implies a highly open heart. This aura hue may be readily impacted by one's neighbourhood or other people, making edges crucial.

PINK

If you have pink in your aura (the second hue connected with the heart chakra, along with green), you live from the heart. You're "caring, loving, and kind."

Pink, like green, indicates that your heart chakra is open and reactive. Celebrate your caring and loving nature, but keep in mind the need of limits.

BLUE

Blue in someone's aura indicates a strong mind. Those with a lot of blue in their aura "operate more in the mental worlds," and must remember to ground themselves. They can, however, be uncommonly perceptive.

Blue is the hue associated with the throat chakra, which control expression and integrity. This chakra is a bridge between the heart and the intellect: it represents the equilibrium between emotions and ideas. If your throat chakra is clean and flowing, the blue in your aura is the external representation of your inner knowledge. It is linked with communication, speaking, listening and authentic self-expression.

PURPLE

Purple auras attract a lot of attention since they are connected with tremendous intuition and sensitivity, as well as vast mental profundity.

Purple is the hue related with the third-eye chakra, which control intuition. Purple in your aura suggest that may be a psychic empath or have intuitive talents.

WHITE

Concentrations of white in one's aura are less common. However, if you do, a white aura indicates a highly fast mind - as well as a tendency to excellence and stable energy.

White color is associated with the crown chakra, which connects us to universal energy and holiness. If you see it in your aura, it may signify that you have a strong connection to something bigger than yourself.

BLACK

If you have black or extremely dark regions of your aura, this isn't the "color" of your aura but rather a message that a part of you is drained or fatigued.

In this scenario, take some time to ground, repair, and balance your energy levels illuminate that aura and restore harmony to your energetic field and chakras.

RAINBOW

If you have a rainbow aura with more than two colors, it's an indication that you're in the midst of a hectic moment or a major transition.

When your aura emits rainbow energies, you may feel particularly motivated and confident, so take advantage of it by going out there and meeting new people and doing new activities. At the same time, this crowded energy can lead to exhaustion and overwhelm, so try to find some time to relax as well.

INTUITION

Intuition is a type of information that comes in awareness without conscious thought. It is not a mystical ability, but rather a capability of the unconscious mind to generate hunches by swiftly sifting through prior experience and accumulating knowledge.

Intuition, sometimes known as "gut feelings" arises holistically and quickly, with little knowledge of the underlying brain processing of information. Scientists have frequently proved how information may enter the brain without conscious knowledge and impact decision-making and other behaviors.

But, where does intuition come from?

Psychologists think that intuition is based on pattern-matching abilities, in which the mind searches long-term memory for comparable events and makes in-the-moment decisions based on them. The natural information processing that underpins intuition is visible in the common phenomena known as "highway hypnosis" which happens when a person drives for kilometers without thinking about the activity of driving the automobile.

Intuition is sometimes referred to as "gut sensations" since it appears to emerge fully formed from some deep parts of us. It is, in reality, the result of brain processing that compares quickly observed parts of current experience with prior experience and knowledge, and it is conveyed to consciousness with substantial emotional certainty.

Because human life is dependent on avoiding danger, our mental machinery is constructed to be extremely sensitive to warning signs and to register them before we can identify and respond to them. That information is the result of the brain's inherent negative bias and might appear intuitive. It is not always accurate, however, because the early warning system errs on the side of false alarms.

Our gut instincts are frequently true, but we tend to give them certainty that they do not always deserve. They are more accurate in certain areas of experience than others, for example, in the creation of initial impressions. Intuition is also useful for detecting fraud and other sorts of risk, as well as determining sexual orientation.

Gut instincts can be useful in making complicated decisions. According to studies of top executives, when even after analyzing mountains of data, the knowledge does not tell them what to do, here is where intuition comes in. People frequently claim rational-appearing grounds for their behaviors and do not reveal their subjective preferences for sentiments that occur spontaneously.

Experts believe that intuition, no matter how correct it feels, is more dependable in some activities than others. It can help you produce fresh ideas or new figures of speech, but don't rely on it to grasp terminology, where reflective thinking is more appropriate, or to judge job applications. In many circumstances, a combination of purposeful reflective reasoning and instinctive intuition is used.

Intuition is a way of thinking, and people vary in how much they rely on purposeful contemplation on one hand and intuitive knowledge on the other. Furthermore, persons differ in one aspect of intuitive ability, namely implicit learning, or the ability to absorb complicated knowledge without being conscious of having done so. Furthermore, some people have more knowledge and skill stored in their memory database, which may be compared to present impressions.

IS IT POSSIBLE TO INCREASE MY INTUITION?

The answer is yes, it is possible to improve your intuition. To some extent, intuition is derived from expertise, which is based on tacit knowledge. In order to strengthen your intuition, you must use feedback, comparing the real-life results of situations to the intuitive conclusions you made. Even said, being extremely perceptive in one area of expertise does not ensure dependability in another.

Here some tips to help you strengthen your intuition skills:

1. Meditate.
Silence during meditation and calm, will help you to focus more on messages from your intuition.

2. Take notice of your dreams.
When you are sleeping, your subconscious mind takes the lead, overcoming your busy cognitive mind that override intuition.

3. Try to feel as much as you can with your five conventional senses.
You can raise your sensitivity to your sixth sense if you develop at their best the other five senses.

4. Be creative.

Drawing, writing, playing music are all activities that relax your cognitive mind and allows intuition to emerge.

5. Test your instinct.

Do you have the feeling that this particular team will win the football championship? Are you feeling that it will rain tomorrow even though the weather says it will be sunny? If you have intuitions about what might happen, write them down and check them after, seeing how often they were correct.

6. Consult oracle cards.

Try to use tarot or oracle cards, and interpret the messages by your own, before checking the real meaning.

7. Feel your body.

Your intuition speaks to you through your body, more awareness of it you have, more sensitive you can become. If you feel bad, your stomach hurts, when you try to make a decision, stop and think: is that really the right choice? You can be just stressed, but sometimes you can be right.

8. Change your routine.

Try to do something different, just simply change the route you take for going to work, or take a walk in the nature. Try to take more time for you during the day, or have a weekend out. When you are too busy and your mind is overwhelmed with the same information every day it's hard to be attentive to your inner voice.

9. Feel more, think less.

Your mind continuously thinks, never stops to wander around. Intuition, on a completely opposite side, feels. Try to understand the difference between thinking and feeling.

10. Pass more time in nature.

Spending time in the natural world, far from all technological devices and so from our cognitive mind, can really help your intuition to flow out - like the animals that live in the forest, and use their instinct to stay safe and survive.

11. Learn from your past experiences.

Try to remember a negative experience happened in your past, ideally not so far. Before this thing happened, how were you feeling? Maybe you had a gut feeling that something wasn't right. Or maybe you've dreamed of something the night just before. More details you recall, and more you will get in touch with this hidden part of you, that's trying to keep you safe.

12. Do repetitive movement.

Walk. Chop tomatoes. Play guitar. Repetitive actions can quite your cognitive mind and free your intuition.

13. Try to understand people before you know them.

Try to get the more information you can just observing people and feeling their auras. Then try to talk with them or learn anything about them from other people, and see if your intuition was correct.

14. Read books about how to develop your intuition, or find online programs that help you to have more knowledge.

THE QUALITIES OF HIGHLY INTUITIVE PEOPLE

1. They Pay Attention to and Follow Their Inner Voice

The amount to which an intuitive person listens to the small voice inside of them and acts on what it says is perhaps the most visible attribute of an intuitive person. They don't question the counsel they're given since they believe it's the best course of action at the time.

2. They pay close attention to their surroundings.

They will maintain a close eye on their surroundings and the scenario in order for their gut to make smart and useful advice. All of this observation implies that they have the essential information to make a decision. They may act on their instincts with confidence, knowing that they have absorbed all pertinent intelligence.

3. They Are Aware of Their Dreams

Because intuition connects the conscious and unconscious minds, a highly intuitive person understands the significance of dreams. They understand that what they think about when sleeping might be a metaphor for their deeper aspirations and concerns. They also recognize that dreams might bring answers to issues or other sorts of inspiration.

4. They Are Extremely Aware of Their Emotions

Whereas many people try to dull their sensations or disregard them entirely, an intuitive person enjoys the input they bring. They understand that their emotions contain vital signals for them that can shed light on the course they should pursue. They don't simply have a sensation: they consider what it's trying to understand them.

5. They can quickly focus on the present.

They have a unique capacity to refocus their mind totally on the now in order to shut out any unneeded ideas about the past or future in order to hear and grasp what their intuition is saying. Only until they have acquired a level of awareness they will be able to comprehend the entire message being presented.

6. They Typically Have Optimistic Souls

Intuitive individuals are better suited to digest anything bad that arises from inside before separating themselves from it since they are more intimately associated with their feelings than most. They are able to rapidly learn from their mistakes, which makes them positive about the future. They understand that good may emerge from bad and that progress can be accomplished regardless of how grim the view looks at any given time.

7. They Are Driven by A Strong Sense of Purpose

Highly intuitive people have a strong feeling of purpose in their lives, even if they don't know what it is. They believe they have a calling that they are meant to answer, and they like to press forward with zeal as if to fully comprehend the significance of this sensation.

8. They Have Deep Thoughts.

You would think that someone who follows their intuition has less need for profound study and contemplation. However, it's exactly the opposite: they find it incredibly beneficial to focus their brains on their values and essential convictions. This permits them to further educate and develop their intuition in order to deliver better advice.

9. They Pay Attention to Signs Provided by The Universe

An intuitive individual understands that there is more to life than what we just see. They are highly aware of the different signals that the universe is sending at any given time. Coincidences, serendipitous meetings, and other seemingly random happenings are all seen as meaningful and used to guide them through life.

10. They are aware of what others are thinking and feeling.

Empathetic talents are frequent among intuitive individuals, which means they can sense what others are thinking and experiencing. Their minds are extremely sensitive to the fluttering frequencies sent by other individuals around them, and they use this awareness to fine-tune how they respond in a precise situation.

11. They may easily gain the trust of others.

They are well equipped to pick the most all kind of replies since they have such a solid understanding of how other people are feeling. They can determine how open someone is right away and adjust their behavior to move towards the place that the other person prefers. They are incredibly likeable because of their non-threatening attitude

12. They are imaginative and creative.

No concept is too far-fetched for a highly intuitive individual, and this freedom allows their imagination and creativity to run wild. They allow their brains carry them anywhere they wish to go, resulting in thoughts and ideas that are full of distinct points of view.

13. They Schedule Time for Quiet Relaxation

They understand that in order for their intuition to function optimally, rest and recovery are essential to let other energies, that may cause noise, settle and disperse. They arrange enough periods of leisure and frequently discover that some of their most brilliant ideas emerge during these times.

MEDIUMSHIP

The activity of reportedly facilitating contact between spirits of the dead and living humans is known as mediumship. Practitioners are referred to as "mediums" or "spirit mediums". There are several forms of mediumship or spirit channeling, such as séance tables, trance, and ouija.

Mediumship became popular in the nineteenth century, when upper-class people utilized ouija boards for amusement. During this time, investigations showed rampant fraud, with some practitioners utilizing stage magicians' skills, and the profession began to lose credibility. Fraud in the medium or psychic sector is still prevalent, with incidents of fraud and trickery being revealed to this day.

Several types of mediumships have been documented; possibly the most well-known include a spirit taking control of a medium's voice and utilizing it to send a message, or where the medium merely "hears" the message and passes it on. Other manifestations include spirit materializations or the presence of a voice, as well as telekinetic activity.

A medium can be defined as a type of psychic, but not all psychics are mediums. There are two types of mediums: natural born mediums, who always had this capacity, and latent medium, that develop their abilities while growing up. Mediums use their intuitive power to see events (past, present, and future) and read people's auras.

How can you understand if you are a natural born medium? Look back into your childhood and see if you recognize some of these signs:

- You were scared of the dark. Kids with psychic abilities have a strong fear of the dark that represent an unconscious awareness of the supernatural.

- You feared sleeping alone and had realistic nightmares.

- You had an imaginary friend. This can be a manifestation of a spirit or a supernatural creature.

- You wished to go to religious services or to know about all different religious beliefs.

- You played with objects like Ouija board or tarot cards.

- You used to read books about spirits or supernatural things.

All these are early signs of a possible mediumship gift.

But how can you recognize if you are a medium now, as an adult, or a latent medium?

- See how you perceive people: do you see their auras, or symbols surrounding them?

- Understand how you feel among others: do you sense someone walking in a room without seeing him? Do you feel other people's energies and vibrations?

- Your experience with death can help you reveal if you have this ability: after a loved one dies, do you experience something strange? It can be a sentiment different from sadness as well as an event, like a slamming door or a dream.

- Listen if you hear any kind of voice: it can be an inner voice or a speech that you literally hear and gives you words or messages.

HOW CAN YOU IMPROVE YOUR MEDIUMSHIP ABILITIES?

There are small actions and exercises you can do to open your mind and improve your abilities.

1. MEDITATION

Try to meditate 20 minutes a day and your focus will be totally rebalanced. You will be more open to see what's inside you and let your capacities blossom.

2. KEEP A JOURNAL

Write everything you feel, hear or see in a journal, keeping track of all these sensations. This will help you to compare the future events with your past sensations and understand if your feelings were right.

3. STAY POSITIVE

Avoiding negative thinking and making visualizations of positive images or practice mantra, is a good way to declutter your mind.

4. ASK OTHERS

Try to ask your friends what do they think of the advice you give them. Record them so you can look back and see if they were good ones.

5. LISTEN TO YOUR GUT FEELING

Don't be scared of taking decisions based on your instinct. Try to use your intuition in your everyday life and trust it.

6. STUDY

Reed books about psychic abilities, telepathy, numerology and all these related subjects. Building a knowledge around these themes will help you better recognize your abilities and understand symbols and signs.

7. MEET OTHER PEOPLE LIKE YOU

Find other mediums around you or online, and exchange with them your impressions and abilities. This will help you to grow together and explore new possibilities.

DREAM INTERPRETATION

While there are numerous hypotheses on why we dream, no one completely knows their purpose. Dreams can be fascinating, but deciphering their significance can be downright perplexing and complicated.

The contents of our dreams might vary abruptly, contain unusual aspects, or startle us with horrific visuals. The fact that dreams may be so complex and engaging leads many people to feel that they must have some purpose.

Notable professor G. William Domhoff believe that dreams have no genuine meaning: despite the uses that human have invented for dreams, they are simply "accidental byproducts of our waking cognitive abilities", but they don't really serve an aim.

Despite this, dream interpretation is becoming more popular. While science has not shown that dreams have a purpose, many experts feel that dreams do have meaning.

"'Meaning has to do with coherence and systematic relationships to other variables, and dreams definitely have meaning in that aspect," Domhoff explained in an interview with the Daily Mail. "Furthermore, they are quite 'revealing' of what is on our thoughts."

"We've proven that seventy-five to one hundred dreams from a person provide us with a pretty accurate psychological image of that person. Give us a thousand dreams over a couple of decades, and we'll give you a profile of the person's psyche that's practically as unique and exact as her or his fingerprints."

Sigmund Freud proposed in his book "The Interpretation of Dreams" that the content of dreams is connected to desire realization. Freud felt that the apparent content of a dream, or the actual visuals and actions of the dream, worked to conceal the latent content, or the dreamer's unconscious desires. Freud also defined four aspects of this process, which he called "dream work":

Condensation: In a single dream, many distinct thoughts and concepts are portrayed. A single concept or picture is used to compress information.

Displacement: This dream work aspect conceals the emotional meaning of the underlying material by mixing the important and inconsequential elements of the dream.

Symbolization: This process filters the suppressed concepts included in the dream by incorporating artefacts designed to represent the dream's underlying meaning.

Secondary revision: Freud proposed that the odd aspects of the dream were restructured at this last stage of the dreaming process in order to make the dream intelligible, so forming the manifest content of the dream.

DREAMING OF FALLING

Dreams of precipitate from tremendous heights are prevalent. It is a common misinterpretation that if you hit the ground in your dream, you will die in real life, but this is simply not true. So, what precisely do dreams about falling mean?

Falling dreams, according to many common dream interpretations, are an indication that something in your life isn't going well. It might suggest that you should reconsider a decision or choose a different direction in your life.

"Falling dreams are fairly prevalent. It represents dread in real life, whether of failure at work or in love " Russell Grant, author of "The Illustrated Dream Dictionary", believes so. "Falling frequently conveys a desire to let go and appreciate life more."

IMAGING BEING NAKED IN PUBLIC

Have you ever experienced an embarrassing dream in which you show up at school or at the office completely naked? Don't be concerned. Dreaming of being nude is not uncommon.

Dreaming of public nudity, according to Penny Peirce, author of "Dream Dictionary for Dummies", could suggest that you feel like an impostor or that you are frightened of showing your imperfections and failings.

DREAMS OF BEING PURSUE

Dreams of being hunted by a known or unknown assailant may be very scaring. And many individuals have these kinds of dreams. But what do dreams of being pursued reveal about your mental state?

According to dream interpreters, such nightmares indicate that you are attempting to escape something in your daily life. According to Tony Crisp, author of "Dream Dictionary", being chased in a dream may represent a desire to escape from your own worries or wants.

The key to interpreting what such a dream may represent is largely determined by the identity of your pursuer.

Being hunted by an animal may imply that you are trying to hide your own wrath, desires, and other sentiments.

If your pursuer is a strange, unknown character, it might reflect a childhood encounter or prior trauma.

Being chased by someone of the opposite sex indicates that you are terrified of love or are plagued by a prior relationship.

DREAMS ABOUT TEETH LOSS

What does it indicate if your teeth fall out in your dreams? According to Penny Peirce, dreaming about losing teeth can have numerous meanings.

This might indicate that you are concerned about your beauty or looks, for example. It might also signal that you are apprehensive about your ability to communicate or that you may have said something humiliating.

"The true nature of teeth is their power to bite, cut, rip, and grind" she says. "When you lose your teeth, you lose your personal authority as well as your capacity to be aggressive, determined, and self-protective."

DREAMS OF DYING

Death is another typical theme in dreams, and it may be very disturbing. Dreamers may imagine the death of a loved one or even their own death. According to popular dream interpretations, such nightmares signify concern over change or a dread of the unknown.

"Like death, change may be terrifying because we don't know what's 'on the other side, which is why the dreaming mind equates change with death," writes Lauri Loewenberg in her book "Dream on It: Unlock Your Dreams, Change Your Life".

Loewenberg also feels that dreaming about the death of a loved one might represent a fear of change, particularly in relation to our children. A parent's imagination begins to wonder where the younger version of the kid is gone as the youngster grows older. Dreams about death, then, express a kind of lamentation for the unavoidable passing of time.

According to studies, persons nearing the end of their lives and their loved ones have significant and meaningful dreams, frequently referring to a reassuring presence, preparing to depart, observing or engaging with the deceased, loved ones waiting, traumatic events, and unfinished business.

IMAGING TAKING A TEST

According to studies, test-taking dreams are prevalent.

Taking a test in your dream may reflect an underlying fear of failure, according to Craig Hamilton-Parker, author of "The Hidden Meaning of Dreams."

"Examinations are difficult situations that force you to confront your flaws" he writes. "Dreaming about failing an exam, being late for one, or being unprepared indicates that you are unprepared for the demands of daily life."

DREAMS CONCERNING INFIDELITY

Dreaming that your spouse or love partner is cheating on you with another person may be quite upsetting. In certain circumstances, people begin to question if the dream is genuine. Is it possible to have a dream indicating your boyfriend is unfaithful? Or that it is already taking place?

While these dreams may mirror your thoughts of infidelity, they do not always indicate that your partner is cheating or will cheat, according to Trish and Rob MacGregor, authors of "Complete Dream Dictionary: A Bedside Guide to Knowing What Your Dreams Mean": "This is another 'what if' dream - you're pushing the boundaries of reality" they say.

Dreams concerning infidelity, according to Eve Adamson and Gayle Williamson, authors of "The Complete Idiot's Guide Dream Dictionary", suggest concerns with trust, loyalty, and communication in a relationship. "If you or your spouse cheated in your dream," they write, "one of you isn't getting what you need from that relationship right now."

DREAMS OF FLYING

Many people have dreams about flying. Flying dreams may be thrilling and even freeing, but they can also be extremely scary at times (especially for those afraid of heights).

Dreams about flight, according to Tony Crisp, frequently symbolize two quite distinct aspects.

On one hand, they might signify emotions of independence and freedom. On the other hand, they can signify a desire to flee or escape from the reality of life.

"Flight alone is most common," he continues, "demonstrating the autonomous character of flying. However, because it frequently includes good sensations of pleasure, flying may represent our sexuality...particularly components of it that indicate liberation from social standards and limitations."

PREGNANCY-RELATED DREAMS

According to dream interpreters, dreams involving pregnancy may symbolize everything from creativity to dread. Dream Dictionary author David C. Lohff says that pregnancy dreams can sometimes indicate a woman's anxieties of being an unsatisfactory mother.

According to author Tony Crisp, pregnancy dreams signify that the dreamer is growing some area of potential or expanding a connection.

DEVELOP YOUR EMPATHIC ABILITIES

MEET NEW PEOPLE

Researchers have shown that attempting to picture how someone else feels is frequently insufficient. Fortunately, the remedy is straightforward: simply ask them!

Try This:

Begin talk with strangers, or invite a coworker or neighbor you don't know well to lunch. Go beyond small conversation and ask them how they're doing and how their day is going.

Follow individuals on social media who come from diverse backgrounds than yours (different race, religion or political persuasion).

When you're having a conversation, turn off your phone and other displays, even if it's with friends you see every day, so you can completely listen and see their facial expressions and movements.

EXPERIMENT WITH SOMEONE ELSE'S LIFE

Take a walk in someone else's shoes, not simply stand in them.

Attend someone else's church, mosque, synagogue, or other place of worship for a few weeks while they attend yours, or volunteer in hospital. Spend some time in a different neighborhood or strike up a chat with a homeless person in your area.

Consider why someone's conduct disturbs you. If it's your teen, for example, acknowledge that he may be stressed, but go further: consider what his everyday life is like - how long his bus commute is, how much schoolwork he has, and how much sleep he receives.

JOINF FORCES FOR A COMMON GOAL

Working on a project with others, strengthens everyone's individual expertise and humanity while minimizing the differences that can divide people, according to Rachel Godsil, a law professor at Rutgers and co-founder of the Perception Institute, which studies how humans form biases and offers workshops on how to overcome them.

Create a communal garden, carry out political organization, participate on a religious committee.

If you have suffered grief or loss, connect with people who have gone through similar experiences.

PROTECT YOUR ENERGY

Are you easily influenced by the emotions of others? You could be an empath. Here, we look at what it entails and offer suggestions for how to prevent being overwhelmed.

Empathy is a good quality to have. It gives you the possibility to understand and share the emotions of others, to appreciate what others are going through, and to help them.

People known as Empath may be deeply impacted by other people's emotions, nearly taking on their sentiments. While this has many advantages (empaths are generally highly compassionate and develop strong bonds), there might be difficulties to overcome.

Walking into a crowded space might be stressful for an empath. It might be exhausting to talk to someone who is upset or furious. Loud noises, strong odors, and brilliant lights might all be too much for some people. Even the most gruesome TV episodes, movies, or novels may be difficult to see or read. You may be an empath if you are highly sensitive to other people's emotions and can connect to the difficulties described. To assist you overcome these problems, having certain tools and practices to protect your energy levels might be beneficial. Here are some pointers to get you started.

1. ESTABLISH LIMITS

Having healthy boundaries is crucial for everyone, but it's especially vital for empaths. Empaths are frequently so consumed with other people's emotions that they lose sight of their own. It is critical to learn to say 'no' more often, to know when to walk away from circumstances, and to priorities self-care.

For example, if you have a depleting individual in your life, create boundaries and decide how much of your energy you're willing to offer him. This might include directing him to alternative sources of assistance or just declining social invitations from time to time.

2. EXPERIMENT WITH JOURNALING

If you're feeling overwhelmed by emotion, it might be beneficial to express it in some way. There are several possibilities, but one good method is journaling.

Putting pen to paper and writing out whatever is on your mind may not only be a relief, but it can also reconnect you with your emotions and help you focus on how you're feeling. Start by writing a few lines every evening to analyse the day and any lingering feelings to get into the habit.

3. BEGIN A PRACTICE OF MINDFULNESS

It is critical to understand what you require and to recognize your own emotions – and mindfulness may help with this. Setting aside time to be silent and present, whether via meditation or an activity like mindful coloring, crocheting, or strolling, is beneficial.

This can also help you recharge your energy levels, making you more robust and capable of dealing with the emotions of others.

4. EXPERIMENT WITH VISUALIZATION APPROACHES

If you're about to enter a situation that you know will be taxing – such as a large party or a particularly unpleasant talk – it's worth attempting a visualizing approach. Assume you had a glass wall between you and the person you're chatting with, so that you may continue to converse while being safe from taking on their feelings.

Other visualizations you may attempt are envisioning yourself in a protective bubble, imagining other people's feelings as water that flows over you, or viewing their emotions as a balloon and letting it go.

Accept your empathetic side and appreciate the numerous benefits that come with the difficulties.

5. SPEND TIME IN NATURE ON A REGULAR BASIS

Nature has a fantastic grounding effect, allowing you to clear your thoughts and feel more connected to the planet. If possible, try to spend as much time as possible outside and in green spaces. Taking the time to observe the leaves on a tree or the clouds in the sky might help you stay in the present moment and feel more connected to yourself and your emotions.

6. PREPARE FOR EMOTIONAL OVERLOAD

Being prepared can help you prevent unexpected experiences that can be emotional overloaded. The idea is to keep track of what stimulates your empathetic inclinations and to have a strategy for each of them.

Some of them will require boundary work, while others will necessitate a recovery plan, such as setting aside the day after an event for relaxation and self-care. When a scenario arises, having these strategies in place may save a lot of time and energy. The better prepared you are, the more you will be able to embrace your empathetic side and appreciate the numerous benefits that come with the obstacles.

You have a talent, and now is the time to develop it.

CONCLUSION

This book is not, and cannot be, a satisfactory manual for empath and psychic abilities. All it can do is indicate some directions of inquiries that may be followed with benefits. It will have served its aim if it assists to draw your attention to particular topics that you were looking for, and gives you the motivation to look further and do more researches.

If you are an empath, you will maybe find out some advice on how to how interact with others and how to protect yourself from other's energies.

If you think you have psychic abilities, remember this is a gift and it's your duty to develop them and let them blossom.

There's a lot more to know, and I encourage you to be curious: read books, search online, look video or film about these subjects.

It's a whole complex world that needs to be discovered.

So let your power grow and don't be scared of being yourself.

BIBLIOGRAPHY

Judith Orloff MD, *Thriving as An Empath*, 2019

Christel Broederlow, *30 Traits of An Empath*, 1998

Rupert Sheldrake, *Dogs That Know When Their Owners Are Coming Home And Other Unexplained Powers of Animals*, 1999

Dean Radin, *The Conscious universe*, 2009

Alice A.Bailey, *The Soul and Its Mechanism*, 1930

Upton Sinclair, *Mental Radio*, 1930

Ralph Waldo Emerson, *The Poet*, 1844

G. William Domhoff, *Finding Meaning in Dreams: A Quantitative Approach*, 1996

Sigmund Freud, *The Interpretation of Dreams*, 1899

Russell Grant, *The Illustrated Dream Dictionary*, 1996

Trish and Rob MacGregor, *Complete Dream Dictionary: a Beside Guide to Knowing What your Dreams Mean*, 2004

Penney Peirce, *Dream Dictionary for Dummies*, 2007

Tony Crisp, *Dream Dictionary*, 2002

Lauri Lowenberg, *Dream On It: Unlock Your Dreams, Change Your Life*, 2011

Eva Adamson and Gayle Williamson, *The Complete Idiot's Guide Dream Dictionary*, 2007

Made in the USA
Middletown, DE
22 January 2023